Catch the Light

Selected Poems (1963-2003)

by

Douglas Worth

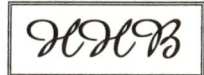

HHB

Higganum Hill Books : Higganum, Connecticut

First Edition
First Printing, September 1, 2004

Higganum Hill Books
P.O. Box 666, Higganum, CT 06441
Phone: (860) 345-4103
Email: rcdebold@mindspring.com

©Copyright 2004 Douglas Worth
All rights reserved

Library of Congress Control Number: 2004002701
ISBN: 0-9741158-1-9

Cover painting: "Catch the Light"
by Patricia Hourihan-Worth
© 2003 All rights reserved. Used by permission.

Library of Congress Cataloging-in-Publication Data

Worth, Douglas.
  Catch the light : selected poems (1963-2003) / by Douglas Worth.--1st ed.
      p. cm.
  ISBN 0-9741158-1-9 (alk. paper)
  I. Title.
  PS3573.O696A6 2004
  811'.54--dc22
                              2004002701

Independent Publishers Group distributes Higganum Hill Books.
Phone: (800) 888-4741   www.ipgbook.com
Printed in the United States of America.

ACKNOWLEDGMENTS

The author would like to thank the editors of the following publications in which some of these poems have previously appeared:

Aspect, The Aspect Anthology, A Year in Poetry (Crown), Blue Unicorn, The Boston Cyclist, Both Sides Now, The Charles E. Brown Newsletter, The Colorado Quarterly, Contemporary New England Poetry (Texas Review Press), Crab Creek Review, Creativities, Dark Horse, Dream Network Journal, Earthwise Poetry Journal, Electrum, The Fathers' Book (G.K.Hall & Co.), Fine Frenzy (second edition, McGraw-Hill), The Guardian, The Harbor Review, The Henniker Review, The Lamp in the Spine, The Logic of Poetry (McGraw-Hill), Longhouse, MAAT, The Massachusetts Review, Meadowbrook News Letter, The Nation, New American Poetry (McGraw-Hill), The New Earth Review, NewMexico Humanities Review, The New Salt Creek Reader, The Newton Graphic, The Newton Library Anthology, The Newton Teacher, The Newton Teacher's Quarterly, The Newton Times, New York Poetry, The New York Times, Nitty-Gritty, The Notre Dame English Journal, 100 Flowers Anthology, Pilgrimage, Poems & Pictures, Poetic Justice, Prairie Schooner, Prophetic Voices, Prologue, Reflections on the Sacred Gift of Life, San Fernando Poetry Journal, Small Moon, The Sparrow Magazine, Spirit of Change, Sri Chinmoy Poetry Awards, Triptych, Trout Poems, The Unknowns, Visions, Whole Life Times, The Windflower Poetry Almanac, and Workshop.

Selections from *Of Earth*, published by William L. Bauhan, Publisher, 1974, are reprinted by permission of Douglas Worth.

Selections from *Invisibilities*, published by Apple-wood Press, 1977, are reprinted by permission of Douglas Worth.

Selections from *Triptych*, published by Apple-wood Press, 1979, are reprinted by permission of Douglas Worth.

Selections from *From Dream, From Circumstance*, published by Apple-wood Books, 1984, are reprinted by permission of Douglas Worth.

Selections from *Once Around Bullough's Pond*, published by William L. Bauhan, Publisher, 1987, are reprinted by permission of William L. Bauhan, Publisher.

Selections from *Some Sense of Transcendence*, published by William L. Bauhan, Publisher, 1999, are reprinted by permission of William L. Bauhan, Publisher.

Selections from *Echoes in Hemlock Gorge*, published by Higganum Hill Books, 2003, are reprinted by permission of Higganum Hill Books.

The author would also like to thank the Artists Foundation, under the sponsorship of the Massachusetts Council on the Arts and Humanities, for the encouragement of a fellowship received during the writing of some of these poems, and the Massachusetts Arts Lottery Council for a grant awarded in 1983.

CONTENTS

From **OF EARTH** (1974)

Cupid 3
Eve 4
Affair 5
Marriage 6
Snapshot 7
Divorce 8
Maple 9
Death of the Past 10
3/21 11
Unlikely Places 12
When You Come into a Room 13
The New 14
Moment 15
Touching 16
Coming 17
Cocoons at the Window 18
Gift 19
Announcement 20
Penny Balloon 21
Poem for Brooke/Daddy/Dad 22
Looking at Houses 23
Psychology of Learning 24
Star 25
Evolving 26
Barrage 27
Father and Son 28
Sidewalk Duty 31
The Whistle 32
Profession 33
Icarus 35
War Bride 36
Medal of Honor 37
After the Homecoming 38

Anniversary 40
Vezelay 41
Excavation 42
Poem on my Thirty-Third Birthday 43

From **INVISIBILITIES** (1977)

Quest 47
Self-Portrait: Writing 48
Worlds 49
Progress 50
Early Nomadic Animal Art 51
The Message of the Senoi 52
The Summer House 54
Guests in Eden 56
Return 58
Waking 59
Deer Crossing 60
"The Small Nouns" 61
Snowdrops 62
Sea-Challenger 63
Grown-Up 64
Da Nang 65
Christmas 66
Republic 67
Lincoln to JFK 68
Dreamers 69
The Task 70
Michelangelo 71
Elegy 72
Other 76
Breakthrough 77
Fountain 78
Transfiguration 79

From **TRIPTYCH** (1979)

The Seventh Dawn 85
This 87
Godfather 88
Revolutionary Agenda 89
Hospital Window 90
Moments 92
Mary 93
The Angel to Joseph 94
The Wise Men 95
2 Walking 96
The Meaning of Life 97
Invitation 101
Easter 102

From **FROM DREAM, FROM CIRCUMSTANCE** (1984)
  Dreams to the Wind

Once I Wanted to Save the World 105
No! 107
The Truth about War 109
Checkpoint 110
"This Land is Your Land 111
The Big Apple 112
Biking to Work 113
New Age 114
Let's Pretend 115
Kite 116
Ghostly Valentines 120
Prothalamion 121
Flowers 122
Windmills 123
Three Tries at a Toast 125
On Schedule 127
A Poem on Spring 129
Fresh Cause for Song 131

Bearing Witness 132
Big Meadows 133
Maybe We Had To Come This Far 134

From **ONCE AROUND BULLOUGH'S POND** (1987)

February 25 137
February 27 139
February 28 140
March 2 141
March 4 143
March 7 145
March 8 146
March 12 147
March 14 148
March 19 150
March 21 151
March 23 152
March 24 153
March 26 155
March 28 157
March 30 159
April 2 160
April 4 162
April 6 163
April 8 164
April 11 165
April 14 167
April 18 170
April 20 171
April 22 172
April 24 173
April 25 175
April 28 176
April 30 178
May 2 179

From **SOME SENSE OF TRANSCENDENCE** (1999)

Middle Age 183
Old Wine 185
Triptych 186
Ascent 192
Crucifixion 194
Peace Maker 196
Bluebird Feather 198
Some Sense of Transcendence 199
Empty Nest Haiku 209
Skipping Sex 214
Butterfly Haiku 218
Angel 219
Little Doug 221
Cycle 224
A Purple Rose 226
Wallowing 230
Valentine 231
Exploring 233
An Ordinary Morning 239

From **ECHOES IN HEMLOCK GORGE** (2003)

Hemlock Gorge 243
Mantra 247
River 249
People 251
Osprey 256
Stone Spirits 258
Praying Indians 262
Sits-on-a-Rock 266
Meadow 268
Gifts 269
Sits-on-a-Cock 271
Stewpot 272
Return 274

Question 276
Look 278
Sawmill 279
Dressed-in-Corn-Leaves 280
Sinking Canoe 282
Gyre 284
January 285
February 286
White Duck 287
White Sneaker 290
Two Incidents 292
Run of the Charles 295
Anthem 299
Fish 302
One 305
Fisher King 306
Vision 308
Picnic 313
Dream 318

from

OF EARTH

1974

CUPID

An arrow has been driven into my heart.

When I try to wrench it out
it curls like a young vine
feathers and leaves dissolving
in my hand.

The days pass
into years.
Inside me I can feel something
healed over
slowly
flowering.

This happens
again
and again.

Once prying open my chest
I found a nest
of throbbing
tarnished pearls.

Sometimes, just walking along
a green wind shivers
the meadows of my blood;
the air grows so lush and varied
I can hardly breathe.

EVE

About her ripeness hangs
palpable, aching to bruise.

Too close you could not breathe
you would have to crush all distance

until you felt that stain
of sweetness flood your bones

drowning in which you would drift
forever, lost, blessed, dust.

AFFAIR

The table cleared
she brings in coffee
and to make the bringing special
a ginger jar.

Empty
even of fragrance
it holds up
under the lamp

a childlike pattern
of blue and red
flowers
which we enjoy, imagining

not a meadow, but maybe
a sideporch garden
on an afternoon
without wind.

Come from her hands
for my delight
it fills up slowly
from inside.

We look on
in silence, sipping
at what
we can't say.

MARRIAGE

We could see it coming
on the horizon
a brightening

that rose, flawless
pointing
toward noon.

Lying, our eyes
half closed
in the meadow

its radiance
was too great
to look upon.

Veering, it left
a reflection, shaving
by which thin light

even the closets
we were going to paper
with roses fade.

SNAPSHOT

My thumb's pressure
in the tack, still holding

it curls
like an exhausted leaf

all but the features, still smiling, lost
and they a bit
distorted, as if suffering
the tension of being
committed too long to a passing
season

the eyes especially, those quick
naked creatures, caught by the flash
at the edge of their dark lives
ache
to be gone.

DIVORCE

For years the bones of some animal
lay rotting, wedged
somewhere inside the wall
of your smile.

Now all that's gone.
The professionals, who can do anything
have cleaned up
in time for lunch.
A fine dust settles over everything.

Still swallowing loose threads
of blood, paper roses, scraps of fresh cement,
you feel the side of your face
coming back
as through a thinning mist
the pain like an angry sun
begins to spread.

MAPLE

as if
burning
old love letters

one could empty the heart
of its weight
of yellowed dreams

and sleep
bone clean
and waken green

DEATH OF THE PAST

At home
more white stands out
in a room

a chair is scraped from the sun
a bowl brought out
then put away.

After a time
a stranger's clumsiness
the look of a day

invites us to believe
we have come far enough
alone, and to what end?

3/21

not yet
the paths
glazed slush

long grasses, heavy
as women turned
in sleep

the sun a hard
orange thought
on the horizon

Nothing sings above
the sound of water
gnawing chains

but an early
redwing hunched
in bare branches

making husky
overtures
to spring.

UNLIKELY PLACES

ambivalence
as a way
of life

Everybody showed up
for the party
but no one was there.

speech where only lips open
sailing the shallows
of each other's eyes

Here and there
a word, a glance
thrown out in unlikely places

claws through
layer on layer of darkness
to admit one barb of sun

shudders
cannot draw back
its root.

WHEN YOU COME INTO A ROOM

The season
does not change.

The flowers, leaning in vases
do not suddenly revive.

Yet, something
in the quality of light

shifting with the eyes' focus, heightening
to new acuteness

harmony
of air and object, motion and repose

becomes apparent
that was not

while you were in the hall
or on the stairs.

THE NEW

It breaks within, shivering
bone of the past
to a maze of troubled mirrors.

A stillness forms, a silence
of arrival.

At every hand
the hard glint
of a diamond

chastens our turning
away.

MOMENT

you stand wearing sunlight
around you
the room dissolving

TOUCHING

husks of defeat
snarled logics
of denial
drawn slowly
under

the body a wakening
field
of desire
each bud, leaf tip, swollen
light films every edge

COMING

the contours of self
give way

clouding

as river
enters river

COCOONS AT THE WINDOW

All winter, ghostly
fists
of summer
they tapped the pane

crusted with a thick
glaze of snow
buried
a month ago

in our minds
another
promise that had not
borne fruit.

Tonight, floating
above the sill, the wings
still
tender with sleep begin

to stiffen, trembling
as when wind
shivers the skin
of a sail.

GIFT

My hand held out two plums
both swollen with sweet juice
one half-a-mouthful bigger.
We had been walking long
uphill, through dust and stone.

It was the slightest flicker
your hand made toward the one
in settling on the smaller
that let me know your thirst

the scarcely-broken arc
between pleasure and pleasure
that left me with a gift
beyond all measure.

ANNOUNCEMENT

Two nights ago
cradling packages
I dropped a fifth of Scotch
all over the driveway.

One picture shows a fish
with toes, another
an egg proceeding on course
through the left horn of a ram.

A poet, I'm supposed
to capture these things
and I try

but the images
nibble my fingers and scoot
the meanings swarm
off the page.

PENNY BALLOON

Two inches tall today
already stretching sleepy
miraculous fingers, toes
in your dark cradle, lined
with softest weaves of our love

even now, lulled in the warm
lap of your mother's blood
in your penny balloon you ride
beyond us, preoccupied
with all you must do to survive.

POEM FOR BROOKE/DADDY/DAD

You addressed your father as Father
complying with that strict male wish
for greetings, departures:
a faint peck on the lips —
like wolves, a kind of polite
throatbaring.

In high school, when I tried
lopping off Daddy to Dad
you went along.

Later, signing long family letters
from Africa, then Trinidad
full of the secret lives
of insects and birds
you had three labels to pick from
under Love.

Home, between marriages, for two days
I came down after a long, rough Christmas Eve
to find you alone
in the living room reading the funnies.
You rose as I came
wordlessly hugged you
kissed you on the mouth.

LOOKING AT HOUSES

Who is it running
through my head
from the door to that bush?

the living room, as we enter, in half-light
familiar
the heavily polished
piano, listening

upstairs, the master
bedroom, small for us, slightly
awesome
the door to the attic
cracked open

on the screened porch, someone has left
a pitcher of melting
ice cubes, mint faintly
breathing

the backyard a dream
of sunlight
and there
peering out from the roses
a stranger's face
with my eyes

PSYCHOLOGY OF LEARNING

Buried all afternoon in Hamachek's
Human Dynamics in Psychology and Education
I look up as Karen comes in
with three tomatoes from the garden.

Soaking my eyes, I sniff
their brilliant ripeness.

Christ! she has grown these
from that strip of dirt
by the garage.

Cleared, faintly luminous
I plunge back into
"The Deterioration in the Quality of Life Hypothesis."

A month from now
she'll walk in
and hand me you.

STAR

Radiant Lady, Love, Karen, how far
since yesterday — now everything we are
washes, is washed by light from this new star.

Lifting him from your arms, cradling him so
I cannot tell and have no need to know
where his warmth ebbs, yours, mine, begins to flow.

EVOLVING

here on my lap, as on some shore
at foam's edge, moist with darkness
life, new life
evolving, dimly casting about
in air

love, like new mountains
heaved out of the earth
above us, jagged, uncompromised
by the slow sculpturing
that follows birth

slate eyes, still muted
as the dawn
already the brightening
mystery draws you
on

BARRAGE

the constant weight, building
exhaustion

at 5 a.m. thumbs, pins and needles
the feeling you've got his arms on
wrongside out

the point when the quivering buzzsaw of his rage
spewing frayed nerves, grates bone —
when song, when even mother's breast
is no solace, the light gone sour…

"I keep thinking this will all be over
in a few days
so I can get back
to my life."

at the cleaners, remarking
"Well, it's only for the next eighteen years."
the white-haired, smiling lady replying
"Don't kid yourself, Mr. Worth — my boy's
thirty-four next week."

FATHER AND SON

1

Well, Colin, here we are
father and son
alone for the next hour or so
your tiny hands weaving, me at my rhyme
together obscurely borne
on the opalescent, brightening, darkening flow
of circumstance and time.

This morning at six
when I'd changed the latest sopping load
and was tucking you back
into the semi-darkness of your room
planning another hour's sleep for you
so I could do some work,
I suddenly realized I was seeing you
more as some thing I owned
to be picked up, admired, cleaned, and put away
than as a person with a life of your own
and no way of telling,
someone who, given the choice, might well prefer
not to go back to bed
if instead he could watch his daddy making coffee
letting the milk boil over, feeding the cats,
or just lie and look at the frosted window panes
sketching silvery angels around the green wine bottles,
and then come and watch me writing poetry.

2

I remember another study,
the heavy, closed atmosphere, intensity
of adulthood — so intriguing, awesome to me;
long walks through the South Indian dawn,
all pearled about us, shimmering
sunbirds exploding from bush to bush,
coppersmiths in the high, molten leaves
hammering the new day...

so many things in this world
never wholly resolved —
growing, we tear ourselves
from dependence to independence,
from there to interdependence,
and it doesn't get any easier,
each stage ambivalent, incomplete
anxiety threading every bond of love —
and to say, as I did in another poem,
"We *are* one another
we must try not to turn
from ourselves,"
seems right to me still, and yet
we turn and turn
of earth, unable to bear for long
the cold, the radiance of the sun.

3

The light is just becoming,
Karen sleeping two rooms away,
Bach softly flowing on and on.
Again I try to shape words to my life,
groping, beginning, along with you
who lie here amid the clutter of books and plants,
the rich disorder that surrounds my craft,
taking it all in, fussing a bit
when I leave you too long, until I must leave these lines
which have no meaning to you yet, and come
put my hand on you, talk to you, fix the covers, and look…

little other, little one
of us,
everyday you grow
both more and less incredible to me —
how must I seem to you
my head still swimming above you? maybe, each day
a little less unborn, more your newborn father.

SIDEWALK DUTY

Still half-asleep, a blur
of sound and light
the children mill about.

Their brightness wounds me —
I feel like an old man
my scarred hands brimmed with precious
seeds.

The bell scatters them
some to assume
a world created for their blossoming
some to hang back
like riches cast by the wind
on stony ground.

THE WHISTLE

Now it is autumn, scattering over the field
the children at football stop, face into the wind
wind clouding with leaves a moment
losing track of the ball, the goal undefended,
the teacher's whistle, the captain's cry of dismay
calling them back to the game's necessity.

If I were a boy again, I might pay no attention
to whistles and captains, when wind came up
and made a dark game of leaves,
but I turn my head
and blow the whistle, and blow it hard again
as if I could blow the leaves back into the trees.

PROFESSION

1

I teach
English at the Junior High Level
whatever that means

Robin, unfolding
leaf by leaf
Emily Dickinson's seared
luminous heart

2

2000 tons of bombs dropped yesterday
the Red River Delta
running blood
"to preserve America's honor
from stain"

"Kontum will be saved
even if that means
the city's total destruction."

America, how can I stop you
from burying Vietnam
or your elected officials
from desecrating the language
day after day for savage ends?

A poet, I make
a living trying to teach
a handful of your children
something of that labor
toward clarity

which is no instant
recipe for action
but an attitude
demanding what is
ultimately, perhaps
unwarranted faith and courage
faced with the maze
the mystery
of the world

3

Dianne's "We know our world
of imaginary beauty
has failed us."

Keith's "There was nothing on TV
but I watched anyway."

Sharon's *To President Nixon*:
"Sir, do you call cemeteries
peace?"

Julie's "Will the pieces ever fit?
I think they've started
But how do I keep them together?
Tape?
Glue?
No, something stronger
Love."

ICARUS

Below him now in the distance
he saw the diminished figure
turn and come wheeling back

too late
the wings molted
as the young man

exulting, on his own
at last, began
the dizzying plunge.

WAR BRIDE

Clear nights, the massive
drone of planes —
curled on the mat, she hugs
her breasts, singing
over and over, something
about the shining
of new pots.

This morning a letter.
She gathers herself
to read, holds it
unopened:
writing this, he
was alive
his spit in the glue.

MEDAL OF HONOR

March April advancing
while the cherry trees
spattered the hills like shrapnel

for thirty days, gauze
a string of tags
my lips could find no meanings

long mornings
on some valleyside I grew
simple as leaves

watching the planes
through the branches
swarm like bees

AFTER THE HOMECOMING

kept going
by his dream of her
pining
or fed up, even, forgivably
unfaithful,
at any rate, a woman
toward whom he must strive
continually, against diminishing odds

seeing himself
as the hero, passing through, slaying
his quota of monsters, surviving
a goddess' arms, a trek
through the land of the dead

arriving, therefore
totally unprepared
for her strength
the impenetrable dream she had woven
of him as the tide-broken wanderer
herself the haven

what remained of the past
between them, that first night
rousing stiffly
to wag its tail once and die

after the homecoming horns had faded away
left facing each other
ceremoniously at the long table
like guests who have outstayed their stories

like ships drifting crippled
unable to meet
unable to release each other

he mooning down by the shore again
she slowly mounting
the smoothed stone steps to her window
the wreck of her loom

ANNIVERSARY

Even the cross
six feet from where she kneels

bleached scarecrow
in a barren field

seems to be urging her
away.

VEZELAY

Richard, lion heart
come
to lay your sword at Christ's feet

didn't you tremble
hesitate
here, at the last

judgment
where the slaughtered
lamb turns executioner?

EXCAVATION

always
here and there
in the rubble
among the fallen
wheels, helmets, shattered
stone limbs, heads

the delicate
flaming
of a leaf, a girl's sex
millenniums ago
still flickering
from the charred page

in porcelain, gesso, crazed
that apple blossom
milkiness
of a baby's temple

unwearying
flower of light

POEM ON MY THIRTY-THIRD BIRTHDAY

Watching you
drift now

folded
into me

my cradling arm in the soft
flow of your hair

beautiful

the blood still blooming
fading
from your cheek

I cannot sleep.

a son
a house now, land
of our own

Living
in evil times
evil, as I imagine all times
must be evil, and good
beyond reckoning

what does it mean to be
'responsible
adults'?

my presents
waiting
in the living room

seed packets, tools

under the painful gloss
of perfect fruits and flowers
the fine mysterious dust

the shovel
leaning heavily
in the darkness
pointing
its blade to the earth

from

INVISIBILITIES

1977

QUEST

always
about to arrive
elsewhere
than this
obviousness, imagining
marvels unfolding
the sudden
transfiguring slant

surrounded
by the familiar
landscape of things as they are
where one might concede
at any point, finding oneself
in the present, eternally
flowering, withering moment, the fabulous
unredeemed here and now

SELF-PORTRAIT: WRITING

Beginning in darkness
I see myself

obscurely
in the window

become with the light
the world.

WORLDS
(for William Bronk)

Being here
we go on as if
it makes sense

this precarious, wild
sometimes painfully
beautiful act

we perform
over and over, whirling
through space

of tearing down, building
from chaos, order
a home —

those before us, after us
tearing down, building
again

imperfect, fictions
all, yet part
of the one

that has made us
what we are
as if through us

the world is trying
to make sense
of itself.

PROGRESS
(for Alison and Roge)

Is that light at the end of the tunnel
getting brighter
as we grow used to the dark?

We seem to be moving
ahead, but who knows?
who would remember
days spun from pure sunlight and weather
the dance and the hunt
and the strange voice calling
from that obscure cavernous entrance?

Whom can we ask
when even our chromosomes seem bent on
consigning to apes, or to Eden, whatever
grace may have dimmed, then flickered out
behind?

EARLY NOMADIC ANIMAL ART

Innocent of the latest
city craze
they recast plundered bronze
to what they knew

the mountain lion
flattening to spring
the stag's dilated nostrils
sucking doom
were ornament enough
for warrior buckle
scabbard, stallion cheek.

Today, when what's most scoured of life
prevails
in the chic modern
galleries

pausing above
each lighted case, we feel
under three thousand years
of verdigris
the same hot shudder slide
from knotted shoulder blades
to tingling hooves.

THE MESSAGE OF THE SENOI
(for James Moore)

We find it hard to believe them
those tantalizing accounts
we come across now and then
waiting for trains or the dentist
of the Incas or some tribe
like the Senoi in Malay
still living obscurely among us
without locks or the need for locks
and no wars for centuries
and always treating each other
as what we call human beings
by which we really mean saints

but there they are, documented
in *National Geographic*
or *The Times Sunday Magazine*
and we have to accept them as fact
so we do, which raises the question
of who's gotten off the track
and if it's us what can we do
about it, right here and now?

Of course we'd like to believe
that we could live that way too
despite what we know about Nixon
and getting from day to day
and what became of Christ
and what our brothers did
that time to our favorite toy
just as we'd like to believe
in Scrooge on Christmas morning
or *Appalachian Spring*
the whole year round, but we can't.

So in the end we reject them
and not without despair
mixed with a sense of relief
because we had secretly tried
putting their message to work
carried it shyly around with us
for a while, like a charm that frayed
the lining of a pocket
until some crisis came up
and it found its way to a drawer
strewn with pamphlets on meditation
hope for the blind, and such
things as we meant to come back to
once the air cleared a bit

or if there had been no crisis
we thought about less and less
till one day, making a dash
against the light, we could feel it
along with some change and a token
we could have used, slipping away.

THE SUMMER HOUSE
(for Viki)

He never asked
preferring
not to know
why the church bell below his terrace
chimes the hours twice
leaving a timeless space
of silence in between —
the first few days
new to the country
he had thought it strange
that time upon these hills
should seem to stop

but hour circling hour
days, months, years
the fact became a welcome
ritual
part of the rhythm
of his laboring
pressed slowly on his mind
till it became symbolic
of a life
that might have been
conceived in Eden
once between a time.

Now, through the rich
late August afternoon,
a text, notebooks
a newspaper from home
spread on the table
where he sits at work,
he feels the year recede

the slanting light
upon him like a weight
indifferent
to all his years
have still to undertake.

A sudden bell breaks
inward on his thought,
another — vision blurs:
the warm green hills
caught in a flood
of light and music, rise:
above, circling
on weightless wings, a hawk
carves azure endlessly
till time itself
unravelling air and bone
must catch its breath.

Vesancy, France

GUESTS IN EDEN
(for Ellen)

sun-lazing, mornings
looking out
from the high terrace
it is as if
one has not asked too much
has earned
these few weeks, guests in Eden

yarrow sloping to meadow
ash and oak
a village
patchwork of farmland rolling beyond
to a city, too distant to touch us
decorative,
in the sheltering mountains
millefleur walks

but a letter, in dreams
another world encroaching...

what they could see
from the rose-clouded fence:

the animals, flowering
antler, crest, and mane
opposed, proud, violent
slaughtering one another

slow-paced and courtly
the same creatures, caught
in the inextricable
pageant of desire —

inside them, countering

all that peace
the less and less containable need
to reach out and touch, to know
whatever is…

our own ambivalence, taking leave
of the dove-filled trees
the streams, endless windings
through bluebells and raspberries
suggesting what pain
they suffered, as they turned
to meet the unknown
dimly advancing fall

RETURN

The Times feels heavy, day
skids by on squealing rubber
nothing has changed
but flashes

inside us, stars
that still appear
so close our hands
might brush them away

flooding the subway, fields
where we lay and fed
each other's mouths ambrosial
wine and bread

WAKING

a blue that burns
the edges clean
gold running the grain

at the window
a branch
from Van Eyck's hand

smoke winds
the sun shaft
tapestry

dreamwork
too delicate
to sustain

red-eyed
the morning
clears its throat

a savage
energy
grinds into gear

DEER CROSSING
(for Karen)

there
where we've put a road through
and put up a sign

we encounter
the problem

of our being
both in and out
of nature

indifferent
and responsible
to her laws

though for the most part we manage
to avoid it

sometimes at night
the blind eyes, the machine
interpenetrate

'THE SMALL NOUNS'
(for George Oppen)

bird
in the sense of wonder
and recognition

and therefore
an anguished
sense of oneself

alive, among fellow
creatures, precariously
acting and exposed

in a world
of flowering
metals, singing

bird
in the sense
of prayer

SNOWDROPS

exposing, this morning
white tips so fragile
they bruise in wind

do not mistake them

whose ancestors gauged
eons of granite
and harnessed the sun

SEA-CHALLENGER
(for Marc)

Knee-deep in swirling foam
lips curling, clenched fists raised
you watch the breakers glide
and build till they loom like walls
that towering pitch and plunge
crashing against your chest.

Little sea-challenger
sand caving under your feet
how can you stop the waves
that can wrestle oaks to the ground
as they slowly crush and grind
mountains to glittering dust?

But to take such a stance, to feel
muscle and bone and will
bracing, as shock after shock
you meet that relentless thrust
spray dazzling your eyes, on your tongue
the salt of life strong and sweet!

GROWN-UP

like when you find yourself
looking around and asking
"Who the fuck's in charge here?"
and it's you

DA NANG

in the dream I would have done anything
to stay alive

face, our face, we have seen it
before, and now in living color, barbarous
face of the human
machine breaking down

walking through woods I thought
I am leaf, rock, in the wind
it is enough

it is not enough

CHRISTMAS

the children
under the illumined tree

bombarded
scrambling out, shrieking
for us to see

our gifts
ablaze in their hands

REPUBLIC

what had been conceived
as a land
ruled by the people
growing, becoming

confused
by size, sheer number
the machinery grinding, advancing
out of hand

lives mangled
the people receding, caught
in the relentless logic
of their own success

in the wake of empire
bands
of the saved, the eroded
going under, turning

inward, back
to the simple, eternal
light
in the Orient

LINCOLN TO JFK

Does it bloom
in every dooryard, brother
lifting sweet petals to each shower
and after, fragrance so rich
when the clusters brush your cheek
it stuns the breath?

Or does that dream still lie
mutilated, wasted, torn
roots and leaves drifting
in another flood
of statesmen's rhetoric
and soldiers' blood?

DREAMERS

who ached beyond
mere drudgery of subsistence
urging the possible
a little further
than at first it had wanted to go

THE TASK

one day the clear task
unfolding, dazzling, immense
vision piercing the heart
of a horizon so vast even death
would be a kind of success

then months, years, of this slogging
through piled snow, leaves, where the path
keeps losing itself in brambles, and whatever
that voice up ahead is calling, it is not
the sea! the sea!

MICHELANGELO

a little man
disfigured
imagine

the beautiful people
in the parks, public gardens
crowded, at dusk

his dwarfish figure
among them, shouldering home
paint-spattered, searching each gesture

his room, the mirror avoided
before sleep the dim ceiling
swarming with gods

ELEGY
(for Rainer Maria Rilke)

Beginning, on your own
even as a child
you found words
playing hide-and-seek
with things.

Not so much alone
as elsewhere, out of touch
with the others at their games,
missing the ball
you leapt for the sun instead
sinking beyond the fingers
of the trees —
and you found words
that caught the fall
of things.

In class, when they asked for dates
of battles, kings
you gave them the circling
eagles behind time's eyes
and bared a glittering era
with a phrase —
for you found words
that stripped the rind
from things.

Drifting through the conventions
of the days and years,
mealtimes, jobs, fashions, cities
happened to you
though you had trouble remembering
directions, names, and the latest
news never took you

where you wanted to go —
but you found words
that sipped the juice
of things.

One day you sucked the heart
out of a rose;
once the deep singing
marrow from an oak;
one night a girl
burst on your tongue
like a burning seed —
you had found words
that plunged to the core
of things.

Unsatisfied, your thirst
for discovery grew so great,
abandoning earth, you soared
up to the dim cathedral
of the heavens;
advancing, star by star
you sensed the invisible
presence of awesome powers
pervading, ordering, binding
the universe,
and called them angels, beyond us
flowing in pure
unalterable perfection
as veins through alabaster
next to those
threading the softer white
of a woman's wrist —
and you found words
that bowed before the mystery
of things.

Chastened, you returned
to the familiar
seamless face of things,
letting them dwell and be
inside you, shining
more sweetly for their corrupt
mortality — leaf, wing, stone
transfigured, radiant, each
a little sun,
that had not been
and never would be again,
caught up by forces, flung
on some fathomless journey
blindly, each in its time
adding irrevocably
its tiny sum
to the infinite
flowing of eternity —
and you found words
that praised
the passing-in-everlastingness
of things.

One day they came, lamenting
that you had died
and bore away a shell
and were satisfied,
but you had left them the living
fruits of your eyes
for all who would come
and like you, reaching, try
the mingled tastes of earth
and paradise,
and gone on ahead —
and you found words
that were not words for things
translations, but things themselves

speaking their native tongues,
and became one with them
beginning again.

        Vesancy—Muzot—Raron

OTHER

looms on the horizon, radiant
angel or demon
of infinite possibility advancing

till half-blinded, trembling, limbs aching
to turn, to reach out
new leaves

we stand gazing beyond
whatever we are
or were

BREAKTHROUGH

that shiver
and flood of wreckage
light, the blind
beak piercing the shell

FOUNTAIN

from dream, from circumstance, what we try
to make of ourselves — that fountain
in the cemetery, the ragged jet
splashing down to the basin, gathered
in a moving stillness, spilled over
clear threads twisting windblown
the chipped stone scattering beads

the art, the disappearing
act of life

TRANSFIGURATION
(for Val)

piecemeal, the world
is falling
in through the holes
of the body
filtered
by the mind and heart
down to that dark
dense core

which opens, or closes
in hunger, sated
nourished, battered
responding, avoiding

riots and roses, sparrows
Mozart, potatoes, murders
crabgrass and lovers

the debris
of days, rotting
scraps of information

sifting, dissolving

elephants, fashions, philosophers
toppling
whole cities crumbling
wars, generations, breakthroughs
pouring in
through the cracks
compressed
silting down

the weight of it
growing, the pressure
building

the small self struggling
to absorb, to escape

and there is no way
out

old civilizations
drifting, the dust, the dreams
of millennia
galaxies

relentlessly
pressing in

till it cannot be borne
or resisted
another minute
everything
collapses
caves in
goes black

black

black

no

something

is beginning
to happen
down there
in the dark

something

has cracked
a crust
seed
spark
flickering
deep
at the crux

is lifting
unfolding
frail
petal-feathers
of light

look

it is the world
transfigured, rising
a new, fragrant
jewel, singing
star

from

TRIPTYCH

1979

THE SEVENTH DAWN

He is still sleeping
peacefully, his face
turned toward the brightening, gleams
as if with its own dim light
as I approach.

So like a god
immaculate, he seems
almost too perfect
for mortality,
his rose mouth fit for hymns
of near-angelic
harmony and grace,
yet sensual, keen
with its lush slidings, chiseled teeth
for the more savage work
of animals.

Curled on themselves, his hands
like petals, acorns
gathering force —
what acts
of infinite precision, reach
ordering chaos
holocaust, may spring
out of their delicate
awakening?

I smooth a curl back
brush the silky bloom
of his warm, sleep-flushed cheek —
his eyes flicker open
blindly, close, absorbed
in dreamwork, bloodwork
flowing beyond my grasp

around the bones
that will support the flowering
of his life
a little while, then fold
and crumble back
to the unconscious
dust from which they rose.

Drawn down by love and fear
for what I have created
in my own image, grown
mysterious and distant
on his own,
ignorant, helpless, and responsible
I bend and gently plant
upon his brow a trembling
kiss of choice.

THIS

unquestioned
unquestioning
mostly, as one cannot
stop and gape
always

reflecting in the middle
of the street, as the light
changes, must
get on with the business
of making it
across

cannot hesitate
to consider
the mysterious
beautiful
lips open, glistening
hungrily
to be filled
with light, cock, meat, drink, air

yet, moments
of awareness, wonder
that it's all here
that we are, somehow
happening, the privilege
unlooked for
wonderful, terrible
miracle

of this

GODFATHER

tough customers, Americans.

"We're gonna make you
an offer
you can't refuse."

a businesslike
ethic
of power

at work
in Manhattan
at Kontum
Wounded Knee

that has permeated
so much
of all we have accomplished

and proven
in terms of what we have
dreamed of
as a people, venomous

REVOLUTIONARY AGENDA
(for Tom)

what one must do
to make it
in one's field

and what
to make it
through the night

a land
where these two thorny blossoms
intertwine

HOSPITAL WINDOW

1

oranges, forsythia
bloom on the sill

2

mornings, the brightly colored
numberless little cars with their urgent
purposefulness
glide along the river's edge

all afternoon raindrops
merge, jostling blindly
down the pane

at midnight the gleaming
hives of industry,
a red light
like a pulsing ache:
Time, Temperature
Coca-Cola

3

oasis
Olympian calm
in the midst of feverish
progress

from which a dizzying
perspective
on what is of importance

should we return…
to rescue, somehow
something…a leaf, going under
the relentless wheel

4

rising at dawn to lean
above the river
returning slowly, dim
as health

drawn by the gulls'
restless circling

there is fear in the question
of what it means
to get well

MOMENTS

flesh blooming
bathed
in a soft shimmering
nimbus

dimmed
by the conflicting
desires, demands, limitations
of mortality

blighted, obscured
by the expedient
abuses, perversions
of this or that system
we suffer, come to think of
as our lives

as if there were no mystery
no miracle
in the clear fact
that we are here, living together
that we are here at all

under the familiar
husk
the live kernel
smoldering
suddenly blazing
out of the dark

MARY

a window
open
so wide
stretching, she burst
into blossom,
light's touch made her heavy
with ripeness

so that the ghostly radiance
spreading its seed
inside her, for a moment
could not distinguish
her flesh from its grace
was just barely able
to tear itself out, reascend

THE ANGEL TO JOSEPH

As when
amid strewn shavings
and bent nails
some spirit of grace
surpassing thought or skill
informs your patient laboring
prevails
until the work stands finished
luminous
and you drop, humbled, dumb

she is God's work,
and kneels in awe
to her own glory.

Come!

THE WISE MEN

Stiff from kneeling
on the cold earth floor
we rise, groaning, stretch and yawn
reclaim our crowns
and set out into the dark
from which we came

gossiping, swapping jokes, flasks, anxious
to resume the familiar
traffic of the world
where our word is law

relieved to let fade
for the moment, the miracle
of incarnation
taking place in the midst
of animal noises, smells,
our bowed gray heads
charged with radiance
jeweled with blood,
spirit flooding the body's confines
like a star

2 WALKING
(for Danny)

everywhere lethal
treasure—I said, "Careful
put that down, that's dirty, that
could cut you, those
will make you sick."
He said, "Look
at this one, what's this one
Dada? Oo, well I want to
bring this one home."

THE MEANING OF LIFE
(for Colin)

at least that's the lofty title
of the poem I set out to write
this morning at 6:30
based on a dream I'd just had
that seemed to be saying it all

I'd just settled down in the kitchen
at my favorite writing place
the table by the window
with its two or three flowering plants
(the window still full of darkness
the plants looking half asleep)
and was sipping coffee and smoking
my second cigarette
having been interrupted
already a number of times
by Tiggy's comings and goings
(when he's in and wants to go out
his claws in your thigh let you know it
when he's out and wants to come in
he lunges at the screen door
and hangs there, spread-eagled, yowling
till someone takes pity on him)
but anyway, I'd settled down
and had actually written the title
and was zeroing in on my dream
when the swinging door swung open
and in walked Colin, my son

O shit! there goes my poem
I thought, but what could I do?
he's four years old, and I love him
and he loves me, in spite of the fact
(or is it *because* of the fact?)

that we're caught up together in this
incredible family thing
that tears along at a clip
of a zillion miles per second
most of the time we're awake
with rarely a thank you or please

so in he came, in his pajamas
all smiles, and wanting to sit
at the other end of the table
and spend some time with me

I told him about the work
I had to do, mentioned the poem
(he knows that I do that
though he doesn't really know
what poetry's all about
not that I'm so sure myself)
and said, "Why don't you go get a book
or I'll give you a pen and some paper
and we can work here together
wouldn't that be fun?"

but he didn't take to that
so we just sat there awhile
making faces and bits of talk
half serious, half silly
the way we often do
when nothing special's up
and he'd brought his twirly thing
we got yesterday at the circus
that lights up and makes a soft
low whistling sort of moan
when you pull the strings and it spins
so he was showing that off

and after a while, as it seemed
he wasn't about to move on
I poured juice and made him some cocoa
between hot and warm, with the spoon
left in the cup, as he likes it
and we sat and talked some more
about one thing and another
like why such and such is true
and how come this and that?
and what would you do if?
and can wolves or weasels jump
as high as a second-floor window?
and what do trees think about?
and I could feel my poem
slowly circling the drain

well, at some point I made up my mind
and told him I had to work
and that he could go see Mommy
or play in the living room
his bedroom, or the basement
but, in short, that he had to clear out
all very calm and friendly
but firm, and he'd picked up
his twirly thing in one hand
and the other was rubbing one eye
when he said casually, "Dada
do your eyes sometimes start to water
when nothing's hurting them?"

I said, "Sure they do, sometimes sleep
gets gunky stuff in your eyes
and makes them water a bit
when you wake up and start to rub them."

then he said something else
I couldn't catch, but his voice
had gone a bit thick and wobbly
and he was trying to clear it
again and again, with no luck
and I was suddenly listening
and looking at him hard
and finally I said, "Colin
are you feeling a little bit sad?"

his reply was all gunked up
so I said, "Why don't you come over
and sit here on my lap
and we'll get all cozy and warm."
so he brought his juice and cocoa
without spilling a single drop
and we sat there, rocking and rocking
not saying anything much
sort of blooming, along with the plants
and then the window was light
and Tiggy was yowling again

so we let him in and went up
and I washed and shaved and got dressed
and he went in to see Mommy
and then I drove off to work
thinking I'll try that poem
during my free block at school
if I can remember the dream

I can't but I've still got the title
so this poem, if that's what it is
will have to do, and maybe
it's closer to the truth
about the meaning of life
(if there is such a thing) than any
a dream could have given me

INVITATION

nothing one can do
is ever going to be
enough, whether
as son, lover, drudge, parent, guardian
of the Word, the world
keeps coming around
for more, someone is always raiding
the fridge, or trying to
start something or dropping
hints or dead at one's feet, and time is not
on one's side—therefore take care
to love yourself
not least, let the world look after itself
now and then, buy an ice cream, settle back
with a cold beer, take in
a game, get into the swing
of that ass, the sweet breasts
of roses, after all, one is only
human, a puff
of elevated dust, in that shaft
of sunlight the ancestral
bones are dancing

EASTER

Nothing. Good.
We are lost
and therefore free

to begin again
creating out of corrupt
mortality, a vision

of universal
kinship
in which light

each caring act
would outshine
the indifferent stars.

from

FROM DREAM, FROM CIRCUMSTANCE
Dreams to the Wind

1984

ONCE I WANTED TO SAVE THE WORLD

by writing poems of global consciousness
but wherever I went the world objected
to my style, the fuzziness
of my thinking, my simplistic
prognoses, prescriptions, the sluggish, abstract prose
of my rhetoric, the insufferable arrogance
of my savior's posture, hinting around that at forty
with a wife, 2 kids, a house, turtle, cats, a dog
named Rover, tenure at twenty-two thousand a year
and a taste for Scotch and Sunday afternoon football
I'm too comfortably off and conventionally set to start
any kind of revolution — in short
the world didn't seem to want to be saved
at least by me, so I said, "OK, fuck it!" and turned back
to the funnies and flowers
and TV and sex and making a buck and fooling
around with the kids and the dog and helping out
with the housework that never gets done and keeping up
with a few friends and colleagues and coming to terms
with my personal failings and the steady recession
toward nothingness of my hairline and the fact
that this whole business of life, awareness and choice
adds only the faintest trace of sweet and sour
to the otherwise tasteless flow
of eternal cosmic oblivion — and I tried
to stop worrying about the world
that didn't want me to save it, and just be
a poet who writes for himself and God
and submits to *The New Yorker* — but it's hard
to completely forget how once you wanted
to save the whole fucking world
when, despite everything, you still do
and wherever you go you hear, "Save me!"
"Save me!" "Save me!" till you say
"OK, I'll try, but don't expect too much

and remember, this time you asked for it, didn't you? didn't you?"

NO!

Because the horror
and suffering
would be

beyond anything
we can grasp
and no image could touch

the sheer waste and loss
of so much
we and nature have tried,

approach some small commonplace
tangible thing
like a flower

and bending
to take in its loveliness
become

for a moment
petaled and open
languorously

spreading your fragrant
silkiness
to the sun,

and in the midst
of blossoming
feel yourself suddenly

flare, crumple, feather
and scatter
as ashes forever —

then try to come back
from that shriveling
instant of vision

without saying No!

THE TRUTH ABOUT WAR

As only survivors
come back to talk about it
and having just visited
they don't really count

if you want to get closer
to the truth about war
seek one who stayed on
forever — go down

past chiseled
abstractions, gnawed
boards, fraying
cloth and skin

to where worms are quietly
tearing the lips
from the non-partisan
friendliness of the grin

and see if the echo
of anthem, shriek, or moan
ruffles that fixed neutrality
of bone.

CHECKPOINT

Make way for the great
wildly-elbowing
human race

running blindly
out of energy
time and space

toward the finish
where there will be laurels
and baskets of sweet

deformed, starving babies
strewn
at the victors' feet.

"THIS LAND IS YOUR LAND

for as long as grass shall grow
and water flows"

you promised
in writing
a century ago

but the yellow
metal that makes you
crazy was stronger.

Now the blue-playing rivers
you harnessed lie blackened
in pools, or crawl barren
in chains through the broken
hearts of a thousand cities

the grass has gone under
a crazy golden
ocean of greed flowing over
the bones of the green-waving prairies
you cleared for your harvest.

This land
is *your* land now, truly, the old broken
promise fulfilled.

THE BIG APPLE

Somewhere, buried
at the core
of all that incredible
crush of stone, steel, glass
and living flesh

a little girl
is eating
strawberry shortcake
on the uptown
double-A train

whipped cream
all over her chin,
grinning back at two strangers,
and calling out, "Mira!
Mira!"

to her father
who is gazing
down at the big apple
of his dreaming
eye.

BIKING TO WORK

The birds are still out there
singing at 7:30
to beat the band, the chill, the smog, whatever
their reasons, along with those long-forgotten
slow-moving, fog-eyed houses, dew-jeweled lawns
leaf smells pungent as childhood
joys and anguish, as you come riding
to ball games, frog ponds, math tests, first loves, riding
legs and heart pumping, cresting a rise
to, gasping, let go, wind roaring, plunging
down the sweet curve of the Earth's breast, flying
out with the sun forever, atoms tingling,
into your life, before glass and steel
sealed you off, domed you, feeding you packaged bits
of the latest disasters, prices, hits
commercializing your options, blunting your sense
of miracles throbbing around you, but the birds
are still out there, singing
for anyone, free!

NEW AGE

Slowly, the overripe
season's
gold gown, skin

comes rustling
in tattered
majesty to the ground

and the long bone dream
of green
is everywhere.

LET'S PRETEND

"Dada, let's pretend
the floor is the water

and let's pretend
the water isn't dirty."

KITE
(for Colin)

1

All that rainy August we tried to fly
that lop-sided kite—an eagle
with a bum wing
that I kept trying to balance
with torn-off cigarette box tops.

I can still see you
heading into the wind
the kite rising behind you
circling crazily
then nose-diving back to Earth

or sitting half-hidden in meadow grass
the kite in your lap
watching me as I stood
at the other end of the string
in my raincoat, waiting for wind,
suddenly shouting for you
to hold it up and let go
then lunging, cigarettes spraying
screaming for you to come quick!

but by the time you'd arrive
the gust had died down
or the string got tangled in clover
or the box top blown off
or the rain started up again,
and you'd be hot and fed up
and want to go in.

The looks you gave me!
The looks I gave you back!

2

That was the same summer
I was attempting to launch
that insanely ambitious poem
about the evolution
and brotherhood of all things
in the universe,
taking it all the way
from the big bang
to a plea for future peace

struggling desperately
to breathe life
into lofty abstractions,
conceding that I was down
but never out

and finally finishing it
to no one's complete satisfaction
including my own

but defending it on the ground
that its vision was solid
important and clearly expressed
if nothing in soaring
to rival Rilke or Blake.

3

That was also the summer
you emerged as Batman
and I became the expert
on superheroes,
straining my hazy boyhood memories
for bits of Batlore

and making up the rest
whose many contradictions
you were quick to point out
like how could the Batcave
be somewhere out in the country
if Bruce Wayne lived in the city
and needed to get to the scene
of the crime at a moment's notice?

Hours and hours you spent
in your improvised mask and cape
trying to get your new image
off the ground
flinging your Batrope's hook
up to the bars
outside the bathroom window
then clambering up the wall
halfway, suspended there
checked in mid-flight, but resolved
not to drop till your hands gave out!

4

Since then you've gone on
to Spiderman and other challenges
such as reading and learning to walk
by your hands across the top
of the backyard swing set

and my recent aerodynamics
in poetry
have involved the less cosmic
if no less high-minded realm
of humanity's need to set out
toward a new age.

We never did get that damn kite up
to stay,
but all those uncertain days
of common struggle
hope and disappointment,
illuminated by flashes
of partial success,
drew us closer together
than we'd been before

and may have helped us a bit
to see and accept ourselves
and our limitations
as fellow mortals
crashing as superheroes
while proceeding, anyway
in that lop-sided, crazy fashion
of human beings spreading
their dreams to the wind.

GHOSTLY VALENTINES
(for Danny)

Down on the high-school football field with you
toward dusk, still savoring the last trace of sweet
mid-February sunlight, it was cold!
I jogged in place, clapped my mittens, shivering
as I watched you climb the chain link fence, snagged, launched
the ball in a faint arc over the fading crossbar
at your blurred face, till my arm got sore, then raced
the length of the frozen field and back behind
your twinkling heels, having held back at first
unable to catch you at the end. Collapsed
on the hard dead grass, we lay panting, looking up
at silver taking the sky, the floating moon
hurled by some godlike hand, dark bony fingers
of trees, one clutching an empty nest. "I love
this time, the light, don't you?" I gasped, as we wheeled
our bikes together through the glimmering
hush of first stars and lit windows up the hill.
"Yeah," you huffed back, "and Dada, let's do this again
tomorrow, OK?" "OK," I said, "if there's time,"
doubting we would as we coasted home, our breaths
sending ghostly valentines back and forth through the dark.

PROTHALAMION
(for Tom and Maxine)

Now, as before, and after
over and over
reach out and touch
the mystery of each other

feel how it trembles, swells
blindly pressing, yielding
in joy and terror
of giving, losing itself

holds back, while stretching
out to that savage, tender
twining of self and other
rooted, builds

a blossoming archway
that is both and greater
bidding you enter, together
the house of love.

FLOWERS
(for Amy Sophia Zuckerman
July 19, 1982 — December 1, 1982)

We come bearing flowers,
fresh-cut, delicate blossoms,
which are all we have,
along with our tears,
to give

to you, who give more, blooming
inside us, insistent, coaxing
our arms round each other,
teaching us how
to live.

WINDMILLS
*(for George Abbott White, Ann Withorn,
and Gwyne Withorn White
on the occasion of the latter's christening,
June 18, 1983)*

Though my two-dollar poster copy
of Picasso's *Don Quixote*
keeps falling
flat on its sneaker-smudged
sun-bleached face
from a muggy wall
in my sweltering
junior high classroom

I keep stooping
to pick it up,
tenderly, lovingly
wiping it off
with damp paper towels,
and with little loops
of fresh masking tape
resurrecting

and sending the chronic dreamer
on his way,
grimed but undaunted,
singing, eyes heavenward, heedless
of Sancho's sputtered appeals
to reality,
armed with bright shafts
of June sunlight
that stab through the half-closed blinds

tilting at shadows, students
in their fashionably labeled
armor, moldering

grammar lessons scrawled
on the blackboard, headlines
from the President's latest
pitch for America

and whatever other
innocuous modern guises
evil assumes
that appear in his path
like windmills
to challenge him.

THREE TRIES AT A TOAST
(for Phil)

Here's to your first million by 40
your mug on the cover of *Time*
phone calls from Johnny Carson
and the White House
and the chance to refuse
an interview in *Playboy*...

Oh, that would be nice

but could you, who have chosen
your work from love of creating
beautiful things,
conquer the world, unstained
by its cutthroat power plays
for fame and fortune?

Then here's to the threadbare craftsman
of beauty, constantly driven
from dinner or bed to labor
in solitude
till the heart of his vision
flutters to life in his hands...

Oh, that would be nice too

but could you, who have chosen
a wife and a family,
be a slave to the muse
and honor the often mundane
demands of love,
fill pockets and cavities
with silver of inspiration
and cover the mortgage with dreams?

So here's to compromising
between those two tempting
stereotypes of success —
a toast from a fortyish
romantic, married, moderately successful
schoolteaching poet's heart:

may you fail to bring in that million
and still make a living from art.

ON SCHEDULE

By noon the rain that had been scheduled
to drift out to sea had thickened. Soon it turned
sleet gray, then more and more heavy flakes mixed in
till someone, looking up, announced, "It's snowing!"

Nothing much more got done all afternoon
or if it did our hearts weren't really in it
as we watched the world turn white, staring like cows
at magic quietly falling out of the sky.

Three inches later, at dusk, the stuff still piling,
the forecasters, their snowy feet in their mouths,
looking sheepish, anxious to salvage what they could
of their reputations, were calling for a whopper.

All evening by the fire we had visions
of being snowbound, sledding, making popcorn —
a day of grace when everything could happen
that our normal, busy schedules wouldn't allow.

Toward midnight, taking one last doubtful look
at the fairy maple, the sagging wires, the birch
that had nearly snapped in the blizzard three years ago,
we snuggled under the covers and fell asleep.

At four, trying to pinpoint what was wrong
I heard through the sifting darkness at the window
a steady, harsher pelting — refusing to look
at the senseless violation, I dozed till dawn

and dreamed of a girl in college I never slept with
who was saying goodbye; then played out several scenes
of things I'd scheduled for the coming day
and hadn't prepared for, each a tragic farce.

At six I met the maple's nakedness
head-on, with a little sobbing laugh, went down
made coffee, glanced through the paper, and shoved off
for work, through a slush of dreams, on schedule.

A POEM ON SPRING
(for my poetry class)

This morning it was so nice
I took you out
into the late March landscape
still half-asleep, dreaming of green
in search of images
for a poem on spring.

"Listen!" I said, pointing
to a song sparrow in a bare bush.
"Look!" I said, bending
to a wall where dandelions
would bloom in a week or so.
"Come on, people, concentrate!"

But, clearly, we were too early
for the flower-crowned god,
and mostly we just wandered
the school grounds, chatting and joking,
glad to be out of the stuffy
classroom, in sun and air
with the moist earth under our feet
beginning to yield

though some of you took notes dutifully
and a few seemed inspired

and when I saw Lenny and Anthony
whacking a tree with sticks
like two woodland priests, after winter
rousing the sap,
I felt something stir, gather, rise
brimming over, as Mandy and Maribel
at the top of a hill
stretched out their arms and came whirling

around and around
down slowly toward me, beautiful
as any blossoms I've seen.

FRESH CAUSE FOR SONG
(for Isidore)

The poems you read
half-speech, half-singing
about being old and still
"the tree itself;"
your stillness, listening, head in hands,
as we took turns trying our own;
your eyes upon us, gentle as morning sunlight
coaxing a hidden animal, a leaf...

There's a picture I'd like to show you
in my wife's parents' house
of an old man out for a walk on a cloudless night —
he has stopped to admire the stars
and stands propped on his cane, when suddenly
taken with wonder, he sweeps his hat from his head
and greets the universe—in reply one star
comes tumbling into his bowler's upturned brim.

Old man, wearing so lightly
in what so often seems a darkening world
impeccable grace and courtesy
fresh as the cornflower in your buttonhole,
still turning up, at 82,
from the rubble of dreams and sorrows
that can choke a life
fresh images of delight, fresh cause for song.

BEARING WITNESS
(for Gary)

Imagine a world
with no one to stop and say
in a breathless whisper, Look
at that sky, that peak, that lake, that tree, that face —
how incredibly
vast, lofty, blue, brilliant, luminous
it is!

If nature means anything by us
it must have to do with this
beholding of wonders
and speaking them out,
that some creature stand up
to testify to the whole
unfolding wrought richness.

Others can stare,
can cry out in pain, terror, ecstasy
crow and keen,
but who else, gazing, can speak
words that move deeper
than sound, than light
into the dumb, mysterious
soul of a thing?

Imagine a world
silenced of awe forever, endlessly drifting
through the dim heavens, a speck
of flowering stardust
full of miracles, blossoming, passing
where no finger points,
no voice rises up
bearing witness.

BIG MEADOWS
(for Bill)

In the meadows at dusk, a sickle moon just starting
its long, slow swing through fields of ripening stars,
sparrows and doves send forth their drowsy hymns
to the last light, through air gone thick and sweet
with clover, clouds of yarrow. Ahead on the path
a shadow darts and rustles, becomes grass.

We search out the richer brown of grazing deer,
approach till their heads, still munching, lift and stare,
step closer, drawn till the invisible threads
of wonder and fear that bind us, tightening, snap
and they turn, leap, bounding away, the white flames of their
    tails
flashing, flickering, fading into the brush.

Somewhere deep in the encircling woods,
dark as a legend sleeping in our blood,
a black bear blinks, yawns, spreads enormous paws,
nuzzles her cubs awake, heaves from her den,
rears her majestic bulk to sniff the air
and rolls like distant thunder slowly toward us.

It is time to head back to campsite, lantern light…
still we linger, bending for one more handful of berries,
perching on boulders, our voices measured, low,
pointing out stars and silhouettes of trees,
then lapsing, mute, into the settling hush,
our faces featureless as worn, pale stones

our gaze spanning miles, millennia, faintly lit
with the gleam of hunters at home in the darkened land,
held for the moment somewhere in between
the ancient glittering mystery above us
and the far highway's muffled rush and roar,
the passing sweep and blaze of alien eyes.

MAYBE WE HAD TO COME THIS FAR
(for Irwin)

for this meadow
to pierce us
with such a rush of green

for this faint trickle
of life at summer snowline
to remind us how precariously
crawling we are
on the thin crust of the Earth

for these woods
cool and fragrant, still
with the hush of arrival
to refresh us so, offering
streams for our kneeling, berries
more precious than jewels

for these butterflies
busy with sweetness
resting a moment
unafraid, on our hands
to seem such an honor

for us to want so urgently
to fit in
taking our place in the landscape
as creatures among creatures
turning, not back, but at last
humbly, in praise
to the clear grace of water
the common gift of light

from

ONCE AROUND BULLOUGH'S POND

1987

FEBRUARY 25

Heart tremors. Chest pains diagnosed years ago
as nervous tension. A worrisome fuzz on my tongue
that doesn't get worse, but hasn't gone away, either,
in three years. Waking at four to lie and wrestle
with images: a ghostly flock of missiles
streaking toward me in moonlight; the blossom-littered casket
of the lovely infant daughter of good friends;
strewn piles of tenured colleagues being cut
right and left around me; breadlines stretching like flashbacks
to the 30s; millions of bloated third-world bellies
bursting with nothing; whole harvests rotting in silos;
the President flashing his million-dollar grin
as he hawks his new streamlined military budget
of 238 billion as "minimal."
Balding, beard splashed with silver, twenty pounds over
what I was when we moved from New York to Massachusetts
thirteen years ago, I take this middle-aged wreck
of a body, three or four times a week, after work,
barring colds or blizzards, and haul it out the front door
to jog with Rover up Grove Hill, onto Prospect,
down the hill, across Walnut, and once around Bullough's Pond.

And love it! God, it's good to get out, away,
for a few minutes, to feel yourself breathing, stretching,
an animal, running: bone, muscle, sinew, blood
all flowing together, moving you through a landscape
of slowly circling green, gold-crimson, brown, white,
along with redwings, mallards, turtles, squirrels
wheeling gulls, shrieking jays, the rattling cry
of a kingfisher, poised in midair, about to plunge,
the sound of traffic on Walnut quickly fading
to blend with the rush of water from the falls
that spills the pond into Smelt Brook, while above you
the sky's turning salmon, the trees holding out dim treasure,
as it must have been for the people living here

for thousands of years before we came bearing gifts:
trinkets, guns, booze, plagues, and the American dream
of plenty of land to make everyone rich, which, failing
to tempt them, brushed them aside or wiped them out...

Then back up Lakeview, panting, praying that Sam
the neighbors' Doberman's inside, turning up Grove Hill
and back through the crumbling picket fence into the yard
that a piece of paper we have calls Karen's and mine,
though really we're only sharing it for a time
with grass, flowers, shrubs, a few animals, birds and trees —
at any rate, "home," and ready for anything
from mastodons to the news to squalling kids
once I've showered and fixed myself a long, cold Scotch.

FEBRUARY 27

Bullough's! My God, what a stuffy, senseless name
for a place of such abiding loveliness
still blooming, wild, at the heart of civilization
despite everything: despite Bullough, city hall, me
who've cast around it a slowly tightening noose
of concrete, greed, and chemicals, closing in
but not yet cutting off its breath of life.

I wonder what its real name is — or the one
it had for thousands of years before we arrived
with our charters and wigs and arrogance and ambition
to build a new town and put Newton on the map —
Great Spirit's Eye? Gull's Wing? Kingfisher's Mirror?

Gulls still glide here, and kingfishers hover and dive,
though I've seen more fish floating dead than caught alive
by birds or the kids who still come to try their luck,
and if there's anything here that stands for me
as symbol, it's that hunched, gray, wading bird
who lurks in the reeds at pond's edge, reflecting, gazing
beneath the clouded surface, much as I
try to fathom the obscure soul of America,
in love still, skeptical, but not despairing —
poet and bird in an aging civilization
probing the murky waters of our times
for signs of hope, living images to sustain us.

FEBRUARY 28

Fenced off, with **DANGER THIN ICE NO SKATING** signs.
The pond so polluted with salt and junk from the roads
it never froze over solidly this winter.
EMERGENCY PUBLIC TELEPHONE INSIDE
a little green box. But whom would I call to say
"The pond's dying. We're on thin ice. Come quick! Before
no one can skate here ever, or birds survive
the fish they catch, or fish the waters, or herons
find frogs or poets images of hope.
Before Newton's like that town the paper mentioned
one morning recently: Times Beach, Missouri,
that the current administration has offered to buy
after confirming it's so contaminated
with toxic dioxin, sprayed on the town's roads
for a decade or so, to keep the dust from blowing,
that it threatens the lives of everyone living there;
so the President's generously offered to relocate
all of the twenty-four hundred residents
that the EPA never bothered to warn, though it knew
for years what was happening?" It makes you wonder
what the Chief's got in mind for America
once the entire globe's lethal with radiation
from the holocaust he's assured us we could survive:
free seed packets, trowels, one-way tickets to the moon?

MARCH 2

I found in the library, yesterday afternoon,
some stuff about the Native Americans
who lived in this region. Called the Massachusetts,
(which means "place of great hills"), they settled in small bands
near streams and ponds each spring and stayed through summer
fishing and hunting, planting beans and corn
"when the leaves of the white oak were big as the ears of a
 mouse"
gathering roots and berries, nuts and herbs;
moving on in the fall to be close to the deer they hunted
through winter when they depended more on meat.
It said robbery and murder were rare among them
and that they lived, for the most part, peacefully,
and when tribes fought over hunting grounds or insults
it usually ended when the first brave got hurt;
that they were astonished when they battled the British
by how many could die in war; that it wasn't their custom
to take scalps till we offered to pay for them.
It said that women took part in village councils
and could leave their husbands anytime they chose.
It said stew was always simmering in a village
and no stranger, red or white, went away hungry.
It said they treated the spirits of all creatures,
among whom they lived as siblings, with respect,
begging forgiveness of the ones they killed,
wasting nothing, downing the flesh to the last morsel,
using the hide for clothes and moccasins,
sinew for bowstrings, horn and bone for tools.
It said they celebrated such festivals
as sugaring in March and planting in May
and made songs and spells and chants for every occasion
from warding off colds to making the corn grow tall,
often guided in this by their shaman, their medicine man,
who kept in touch with the spirits that dwell in all things,
created and overseen by the Great Spirit,
and who'd fast in times of calamity to appease

the angered spirits, and make lighter magic
to entertain and charm at other times.
It said they loved dancing and singing and storytelling,
having no written language, tales about tricksters
fables and myths, often spiced with humor and sex
which shocked the Puritan fathers who must have thought
they'd left behind such leanings with Shakespeare and Chaucer.
It said young men, courting, would sing or play their flutes
at their sweethearts' wigwams on sultry summer evenings
until they came out to stroll with them into the dusk.
Some grandfathers still, it said, would sing in the evenings
to their "mountain flowers," their lovely "spirit blossoms."
It said they played football, hockey, lacrosse, and handball,
gambled with painted pebbles, played cards made of rush,
kept dogs for pets, made popcorn and strawberry bread,
and overindulged their kids who grew sleek and saucy.
It said that before we brought in the idea of heaven
they had no conception of "happy hunting grounds,"
finding everything here as it should be. In short, it sounds
like a good life they led for millennia
till it came to a sudden end in the 1600s
through a series of battles and even more lethal plagues
brought over by white men, along with their thunder sticks,
that wiped out nine out of ten of the Massachusetts
in village after village, and scattered the rest.

MARCH 4

Not that their lives were Edenic before we came,
exposed as they were to sudden storms and droughts,
epidemics, wild animals, wandering hostile tribes.
God knows I wouldn't want to have to move
each fall with the deer, or fend off wolves and bear
with stone-tipped arrows and spears — I've got my hands full
with Sam, after jogging, or on my way to the bus
in the morning, when he barks from his yard and comes
  charging,
fangs bared, as I keep on walking, scarcely breathing,
or stop with a prayer and croak out, "Good dog! Good Sam!"
never sure if the sniffing and licking he sometimes does
at my hand's being friendly or whetting his appetite
for the softer flesh of my throat! And the raccoons and skunks
I've surprised now and then at the trash cans at night have
  scared me
far more than I them, I'm sure; and even the squirrels
that plop from the roof to the bird feeder at the window
in the kitchen where I write have given me looks
that made me wonder which of us was at home.
So I'm not pushing the life of the "happy savage"
by any means. I'm grateful for supermarkets
where meals lie quietly wrapped in cellophane;
and where would I be without modern medicine,
having had scarlet fever as a child
and mumps at seventeen? Don't get me wrong —
I couldn't be more delighted with the triumphs
of civilization, from Mozart to central heating,
typewriters to ice cubes. But somewhere along the way
we seem to have lost something, some sense of perspective
and reverence toward nature, toward each other,
where we've come from, that we really are brothers and sisters
to animals, trees and streams, and that we need them
if we're to go on with our video games and computers,
our music of chance, our theater of the absurd,
because the bottom line is we've got to breathe

air and drink water and harvest food from the land,
and if we keep plundering, wasting, and poisoning them
with toxic dioxin, acid rain, radiation,
out of myopic selfishness and greed,
we're going to die, along with most everything else;
and maybe the people who lived here before us had something
that could help us, *save* us, though we nearly destroyed them:
some sense of the balance, the interconnectedness,
the complex harmony of the world, created
by some cosmic spirit greater than we can fathom
but that we can try to honor, as they did
before Lieutenant John Spring built the first grist mill
in Newton, on Smelt Brook in 1731
and cut off the fish that used to come up the Charles
from the ocean and fill Bullough's Pond each spring;
before Bullough, "the ancient proprietor of the land,"
put his shoulder to the profitable wheel
of progress when, quote, "this beautiful sheet of water,
like a sapphire gem set round with emeralds
(was) of tolerable depth and great purity."

MARCH 7

Sometimes I imagine someone running before me,
ahead a few paces, and a few hundred years,
whose people had been around for several thousand,
who knew and loved this pond; someone like me
but younger, who used to circle the pond each day
two or three times, out of sheer exuberance,
in moccasins or barefoot, not having to worry
about shards of broken bottles and rusting cans;
who lived up the hill, as I do, with his wife
and kids and dog and neighbors, squirrels and skunks,
raccoons and flowers; someone like me, but fresher,
more brimmed with the juice of living, less skeptical
about his place and role in the universe;
a poet, no, bard! from whose breast song came gushing
pure and deep and clear and elemental
as blue sky, flaming maple, cardinal's whistle,
yet playful as the iridescent sheen
of a mallard's head spraying beads of sunlit water;
a singer-priest, highly honored in his village
by people living more simply in a time
when humans were closer to birds and trees and water
and profits were edible, and bits of seashell
were crafted and strung in patterns as gifts to wear:
wampum, before we dulled that term with trade.
I'd like to think someone of that sort really existed,
when America itself was younger, fresher,
and call his spirit back and get to know him
as I jog along in his footsteps, but how to address him?

MARCH 8

Forerunner? Brother? Companion? What should I call you?
Running Wolf? Deerfoot?
                                      Bluefisher I am named
after the gray-blue bird who soars and hovers
above the fish-brimmed waters of this pond
we call Earth Mother's Basket, folds its wings
and like a spear-point plunges, disappears
with a splash below the surface, re-emerging
to climb the air again with silver treasure
clasped in its beak. My spirit too ascends
to hang with cloud or sun or moon or star
over the world, looking far and slow and deep
beneath the surface, into the souls of things,
sensing connections, seeing how wing and leaf,
bone and reed, star and flake, standing bear and brave
are woven into one pattern, cousins, children
of the Great Spirit Father and Earth Mother.
And when such vision fills me till I shiver
with awe, delight, and wonder, I too plunge
and, with a flash of inspiration, pierce
the world to its sacred essence, bringing forth
riches: songs, chants, prayers, stories, for my people,
for I am shaman, powaw, medicine man,
healer, priest, entertainer, singer, clown,
man-flute through whom creation's voices flow.

MARCH 12

Little purple flowers, blooming so delicately
among curled leaves, shriveling patches of old snow,
how open and trusting you are, your arms thrown wide,
exposing the pure white innocence of your breasts,
the slender yellow stalks tipped with golden treasure.

Foolish blossoms, shaken by every breeze,
don't you know that Winter may pass this way again
and cloak you in ice and snow? And his friend the North Wind
snap your thin stems and scatter your pretty petals?

Rootless warrior-hunter, stepping so cautiously
in deerskin shoes among puddles and mounds of snow,
how closed and fearful you are of what you don't know.
We were here to welcome the Spirit of Spring
long before the first arrow shooters came,
and we will be here to praise the sweet buds of her breasts
long after the last, cruel, blood-encrusted stone
lies buried deep in the heart of Mother Earth.

Foolish human, if you would call yourself brave,
loosen your bow, cast off your shoes and robe,
fling your arms wide, and as your feet sink in mud
let the cool hands of Wind, the warm lips of Light
play over your breast and the treasure stalk you keep hidden
until you stand brimming, worthy to toast the slim spirit
approaching, dreamily, with sun-drunk sighs.

MARCH 14

Old Stony Coat, ancient ice spirit, lying sprawled
in Earth Mother's Basket, half-asleep, get up!
Up, lazy bones, and head north where you belong
before Spring Spirit finds you drowsing here
and melts your icicle! Up now, drooling graybeard.
You've had the pond all winter. Now it's time
to loosen your cold embrace and let the sun
caress and stir her back to life. It's time
for Gull to bob and drift like a child's birch boat,
and Mallard, with his sweetheart, blissfully paddling,
in a sudden fit of passion, to plunge his head
into the water till only his ass sticks up,
then right himself, and, kicking, spread his wings,
flap furiously, and go whooshing across the surface
in a blur of sunlit spray and gleaming feathers —
while she, for whom this dazzling show's intended,
floats calmly on, demurely tucked, her tail
flicking from side to side to show she's seen
but doesn't think much of such male foolishness.
It's time for Redwing to build among the reeds,
and Oriole blaze, and Kingfisher freeze in air,
and Heron stare at his feet, and Bluejay jeer,
while Mockingbird pokes fun at everyone.
It's time for Fish to flash, and Frog to croak
his passion song at dusk, and time for Turtle
to sneak like a floating boulder around the pond.
It's time for Raccoon to scrub his delicate hands,
and Doe drop down her lovely neck to sip
at her reflection, and Bear scoop fish for lunch,
and Dragonfly, like a tiny, magic arrow
of flame or ice, dart two or three places at once.
It's time for me, the moist ground softening,
to run again, barefoot, round and round the pond,
until I hear Wind whispering in my hair
and feel the hearts of roots pounding under my feet,

blood climbing trunks, limbs stretching sleepy fingers;
round and round, until I am Moon and Sun
circling the Earth as I fly! Up, sluggish one.
Enough of your dull gray glinting. Take off! Scram!

MARCH 19

Rest assured, Little Brother, as you slowly turn
sizzling, we will waste nothing, savoring you
to the last morsel, sucking on every bone.

And when your flesh has become part of us,
we will preserve your lovely glossy coat
by turning it into a hat for our ears in winter.

The wonder of your ever-lengthening teeth
will be recalled for ages, as they click
strung on your sinew, handsomely set off by beads.

Nor will your bones lie idly whitening,
but will keep busy and useful as before
when you employed them: scraping, poking and digging.

Even the finer bits and claws will serve
to keep the children happily at their games
of counting and sorting, rainy afternoons.

Therefore, O Beaver, forgive us, if you can
for taking your life. The Great Spirit made it so
that creatures kill other creatures — but only in need.

A curse upon him who slaughters with pride for sport,
lugging the head home, leaving the carcass to rot!
Come, we will eat you now, properly, with respect.

MARCH 21

Hail, Grinning Fox! Triumphant warrior
of the Massachusetts! You, who clasped the arm
of Courage, and spat in the face of Common Sense
when you flirted yesterday with the pretty wife
of Gray Wolf, who'd come to our village for a council
of neighboring sachems. Slitting your eyes at her
and flexing your muscles, until she had to cough
to hide her amusement, and the chief noticed you.

You, who took such offense when Gray Wolf smiled
at your idiocy and called you a fine young cub
which caused you to challenge him and all his braves
to battle, risking the lives and happiness
of many over a trifle.

                You, who ducked
when the first arrow whistled over your head
and made your butt a target for Gray Wolf's practice,
escaping injury with more luck than cunning
by a feather's breadth, when your shirt was pinned to a tree
by a stray arrow; howling until we came
to free you, and one of our braves started whooping with
   laughter,
and Gray Wolf arrived and couldn't resist joining in;
then one after another, catching the fever,
we leaned on our bows, stamping helplessly, both sides
   collapsing,
thus ending, happily, the whole stupid affair.

Hail, fearless brave! Your grin is not so wide
as it was yesterday. Go now and grow
to be a man who thinks before he pokes
his tongue in a honeycomb. Go, Grinning Fox,
with your head up, lest we rename you Slinking Dog!

MARCH 23

Out fighting with Grinning Fox the other day
to try to rescue the young brave's kidnapped pride,
Mild Muskrat caught a cold, or a cold caught him
as it often does when he overexerts himself,
having, from birth, been delicate, though strong
with a power of gentleness in his hands and voice
for easing the backs and smoothing the ruffled feathers
of many an aching brave or angered neighbor.

Therefore, O Streaming Nose, potent spirit of colds,
both scratcher of throats, mighty piler of phlegm in the chest,
ease up on Mild Muskrat, let him once again breathe
comfortably through the night beside his wife
instead of waking up clogged and coughing his lungs out
until she jerks the bearskin over her head
and contemplates murder or moving back in with her folks.

Look, I have put on my shaman's robe and the mask
with the foot-long, flaming nose, and the eyes gunked shut,
and pounded my drum like a headache's throb as I danced
three times around the village, hacking and sneezing,
to remind my people of your terrible powers
and beg you to relent and leave Mild Muskrat
in peace. If you must plague someone in our village
take Grinning Fox, who so juicily deserves you,
and like you, O Spirit, has proven himself at running!

MARCH 24

Sly Dog, you shameless trickster, beggar, thief,
sniffing around the stewpot at dinner time
as if you just happened to be passing by
tracking a rabbit or squirrel, and suddenly lost it
and figured it must have leapt up into the stew.
And when we sit to eat, plunking your head
in our laps like a gift, looking up with such pleading eyes,
such twitching of eyebrows, high-pitched mournful whines,
we throw you a morsel just to get rid of you
for a moment and try to enjoy our meal in peace.

And if there's no food to be had, it's affection you're after
as if we'd nothing better to do all day
than pet you, eternally stroking, patting and scratching,
pawing at us while we're busy with our tasks,
burrowing under a hand with your cold wet nose
so we upset the bead dish or slice ourselves fixing stew,
and if we've lain down for a little rest, sneaking up
to drench our ears with your slobbery, slug-like tongue,
or dropping a stick on our unprotected faces
and yapping furiously for us to get up
to throw it so you can bring it back again.

Then at night, when you're supposed to be on guard
outside the wigwam, snoring obliviously
while bears swarm by or raccoons scatter our stores,
then waking an hour before dawn when we're still asleep
and baying at some imaginary intruder
because you're lonely, and then, when we let you in,
thumping and snuffling and licking until we go crazy
and throw you out again to bark some more.

O terror of ticks and fleas, we'd be better off
without your smelly carcass poking about —
and yet, last week, when you didn't show up at dinner

and we ate in strange peace and quiet, and you still hadn't
 come
when we closed up the wigwam and lay down to sleep...
we couldn't, all of us breathing quietly,
listening for your sharp yap, the quick dance of your paws
until I got up and went out to search for you
all around the pond, up and down the glimmering brook,
and came back without you and lay down again
hearing the thump of my heart, the restless turning
of Running Deer and Little Squirrel, the sighs
of Goldwing, Cooing Dove squalling in fits till dawn...
when you arrived, softly whimpering, on three paws,
blood crusting your neck and muzzle, stinking of swamp,
and, cursing and crooning, we stroked you, gently, and kissed
 you,
and fed you out of the stewpot and bathed your wounds
and wrapped you in blankets and set you on our best bearskin,
and you sat there, yapping and grinning, you terrible creature,
sassy and proud as a brave who comes staggering
home after his first battle or night of love.

MARCH 26

Once Porcupine had the softest coat of all.
If you don't believe me, tickle him under the chin
until he rolls over and stretches out on his back;
then stroke his belly — you'll find that it's even softer
than Rabbit or Mole. A long, long time ago
his coat was like that all over, so tempting to stroke
that nobody who came near him could resist,
including Chief War Cloud's daughter, the lovely sweetheart
of True Arrow, a fierce young brave in the tribe.
Sparkling as stones in water were the eyes
of Laughing Brook, and sweet as maple syrup
her flowing voice, and she had quite a body, too!
And True Arrow was jealous, crazy jealous
of anyone who even looked at her.

One day, when she was passing Porcupine
who was lying stretched in the sun, she stooped to stroke
his lovely coat, but True Arrow seized her wrist
and vowed he would murder Porcupine if she ever
touched him again. Poor Porky was terrified
and furious, complaining it wasn't his fault
that everyone liked to stroke him. Well, sure enough,
it happened — one day when she thought no one was looking
Laughing Brook brushed her hand down Porcupine's back
as she passed him at the pond. True Arrow's spy,
Raven, observing this, flew croaking away.
Luckily for Porcupine, his friend Sparrow
saw Raven spying on Laughing Brook and followed
and saw True Arrow gathering all his friends
to come and shoot Porky. When the poor creature heard
he fled to the woods, but True Arrow tracked him down
and he and his friends enclosed him in a tight circle
all pointing their arrows at him. "Mercy!" he cried.
"Great Spirit, don't let them kill me. Is it my fault
that everyone like to stroke me? Help me, please!"

True Arrow's heart was quartz, but the Great Spirit,
who happened to be looking that way from the sky,
heard Porcupine, and, softened with compassion,
decided to do what he could. He couldn't change
True Arrow's nature, having created him so,
but as the brave cried out, "Shoot!" and bowstrings twanged,
he turned the arrows, just as they reached their mark,
so that the feathered ends slid into Porcupine
without killing him and lodged with their points sticking out.

And ever since that day Porcupine's gone about
with arrows bristling all over his back and tail.
(They missed his head and neck, which he'd tucked under
as True Arrow's friends let fly. And the tips have worn down,
from rubbing against each other for thousands of years,
to the finest needle points.) So no one can stroke him,
unless, as I said, you tickle him under the chin
and he rolls over, belly up. But please don't try it,
you little ones, unless your mother or father
says it's OK, and you ask him first, politely,
if he *wants* to be tickled. I'd hate for you to end up
with a quiver of arrows sticking out of your hand!

MARCH 28

It's raining again. Running Deer and Little Squirrel
are sitting inside the entrance flap of the wigwam,
Running Deer drawing with a bone on bark
while her younger brother arranges small, smooth pebbles
in patterns. "What are you drawing?" asks Little Squirrel
in a tone that suggests he doesn't want to know
except to criticize. "Is it a caribou?"
As Running Deer says nothing, Little Squirrel
remarks, "Well, it doesn't look like a caribou."
Running Deer goes on drawing. "It looks like a dog
that is trying to be a moose." Little Squirrel laughs.
Running Deer still doesn't answer, though a line forms
between her eyebrows and she works her tongue
harder against her cheek as she goes on drawing.
Then a smile quietly blossoms across her face.
"If Daddy brought back nine deer eight days in a row
how many would we have?" Little Squirrel stops
the pattern he was working on and thinks,
scooping some pebbles up and shaking them
so they rattle in the hollow drum of his hands.
"Eighty-nine?" "Wrong! I thought you were so good
at numbers." "I am," he says, "for someone my age.
Ask me another." "No," she says, "you're too dumb.
You'd just get that one wrong too." "No I wouldn't," he says.
"You're just being mean to me because you're jealous
that everyone says how good I am at numbers
and you're not good at anything at all.
You can't even draw a caribou—look at that!"
"It's not supposed to be a caribou,
dummy—it's an imaginary creature
that can fly, and has horns made of candy, and eats little boys
who try to break off a piece." While Little Squirrel
takes all this in, carefully studying it, in silence,
he spreads out his pebbles in several short, neat rows.
"Seventy-two," he says, after a while.

"What flavor candy?" "Strawberry," Running Deer says.
"But it's poisoned, just in case some boy like you
breaks off a piece while it's sleeping and runs away.
You'd die a horrible death, turning blue in the face
and throwing up globs of green yuck all over the place,
just like you did the other night on your bearskin.
And while you were dying, we'd all laugh and laugh
at your stupid green face." "You just said it would be blue.
You're the stupid one. You're so dumb you can't remember
if something's blue or green. Mommy says you're dumb;
I heard her the other night talking to Daddy about it.
I bet you're the stupidest girl in the whole Massachusetts,
and you don't even have a you-know-what!" "A what?"
"A you-know-what. Down there. Like me and Raven."
"Girls aren't supposed to have them, pigeon-brain,
which shows how smart you are! I bet you think
they're just for making peepee, don't you? Hah!"
"I know what they're for," says Little Squirrel, softly.
"Tell me then. What? Go on. See? You don't know.
Well, they're for making babies!" Little Squirrel
arranges the pebbles into two long lines
next to each other, and answers, "No they're not.
You're just trying to trick me. Women make babies
in their bellies. I've seen them. Like Mommy did this winter
with Cooing Dove…Hey look, the sun's come out.
Come on, I'll race you down to the pond." "OK,
if you'll give me a headstart. Wait, no fair! Come back!"

MARCH 30

Come, Long Nose, children snatcher. Here are two
prime victims: Running Deer and Little Squirrel
who've been squabbling and whining, clawing and bickering
since dawn over who goes first or who got more,
who's smarter, who's stronger, which one the dog likes better,
pestering Goldwing for sweets while she's making stew,
tearing in, shrieking, just as Cooing Dove
has gotten to sleep so she starts up screaming again,
sneaking off with my medicine rattle and drum
when only last week they carelessly broke my bone whistle
and left my best rattle lying exposed in the rain
that came down all afternoon and ruined it.

Come, nightmare spirit, friend to desperate parents.
These two I have here by the ears have been asking for you
to come and pop them into your big pack basket
and carry them off to your dark cave in the woods
and throw them into your bubbling pot and boil them
till all their nasty selfishness is cooked out
and they're ready to be gobbled up limb by limb
till only their bones, hair, nails and teeth are left.
Let's see if they're still arguing then as to which
is tenderer, tastes better, gets to your stomach first!
Here, take them, if you can stand them, and good eating!
I only hope they'll give you less indigestion
than they've given me today, these two spoiled brats!

APRIL 2

Still awake? It's late. No more talking now. Time to sleep.
A backrub? Well, all right. A very quick one. Move over.
It's funny, hearing the two of you laughing just now
reminded me of a time when I was your age
and played a trick on my sister, your Auntie Willow.
One evening, when she had gone out of the wigwam
to wash up for the night, I put a big frog
way down at the foot of her bearskin. When she came in
I tried to cover my laughter with a loud yawn
as I went out to wash up myself. We used to fight
and tease each other at least as much as you two
and Grandmother and Grandfather would get furious
and yell and scold us about how bad we were
and then forgive us. Anyway, when I came back
and pulled up the covers, I lay very still in the dark
waiting for Willow to scream (She didn't like frogs
and hated to be surprised.) — but nothing happened.
"Willow," I said at last, unable to stand it
any longer, "Are you asleep?" "No," she replied.
"Are you?" "Now how could I be talking to you
if I was asleep?" I said. She only giggled.
"Are you comfortable?" I said. "Uh huh," she answered.
"You know," I said, "I like to sleep with my feet
way down at the very bottom. Have you tried that?"
"That's how I always sleep," she said. "Oh," I said.
"Don't you like to wiggle your toes all around down there
and poke them into the corners?" "Yes," she said.
"Let's do it now, OK?" "OK," she said.
"It's fun," I said, "isn't it?" "Yes," she said, and giggled.
"Haven't you sometimes imagined something's down there
clammy and cold and horrible waiting to bite you?"
"I used to," she said, "but now I check down there first
before I get in, to be sure." "You do?" I said.
"Yes, always," she said. "Like tonight, you won't believe
what I found down there?" "You found something" I said.

"Yes, an old frog. I guess it must have hopped in
when Mommy was airing the wigwam this afternoon."
"Oh," I said casually. "What did you do with it?"
"I let it go, of course, stupid!" she replied.
"Good," I said. "Well, goodnight." And feeling foolish
I turned over on my side and closed my eyes.
"Bluefisher?" she said, after a moment's silence.
"Are you asleep yet?" "No," I said. "What is it?"
"Do you ever sleep on your side with both hands tucked
under the pillow, nestling all cozy and warm?"
"Sometimes," I said. "Are you doing it now?" she asked.
"No," I said. "Try it," she said, and let out a squeak,
then a muffled whoop, and even before my hands
started moving up and under, I knew what I'd find.

APRIL 4

Cooing Dove, coo, and I will give you the sun
to hold in your hand and toss high into the air
so that wherever you go will be light and warmth
and your life will be long and worthy. Cooing Dove, coo.

Cooing Dove, coo, and I will give you the moon
on a string of stars to wear round your neck like a shell
so that wherever you go a soft beauty will glow
and your life will be long and worthy.   Cooing Dove, coo.

Cooing Dove, coo, and I will give you the wind
that is sighing for love, to billow your skirt and your hair
so that wherever you go men's hearts will be full
and your life will be long and worthy. Cooing Dove, coo.

Cooing Dove, coo, and I will give you the rain
that is weeping, weeping for all the sad things that happen
so that wherever you go will be eased by compassion
and your life will be long and worthy. Cooing Dove, coo.

Cooing Dove, coo, and I will give you the earth
to live on with all your brother and sister creatures
so that wherever you go you will be at home
and your life will be long and worthy. Cooing Dove, coo.

APRIL 6

To dance the spring leaf, you must be darkness furled
upon itself, for months, then slowly, slowly
feel something deep within yourself begin
to stir, swell, tighten, start to edge its way
outward, toward something dimly felt, disturbing,
intriguing, drawing you further, gently insistent,
compelling, growing sharper till you ache
to stretch, spread, open, give yourself completely
into some softly flowing golden warmth
coaxing, caressing you, until you can't bear it
and burst forth, terrified, into the searing light
crying out something indistinct, over and over
whose meaning you can't quite grasp, but which you keep trying
more and more boldly: green, green! Green, GREEN! GREEN!

APRIL 8

Each day some new wonder bursts upon the scene:
a miniature sun, a bush in purple flames,
a scarlet flash, a golden curl of song,
a rock at stream's edge robed in green, the smell
of rain one night announcing Spring's arrival.

In the village girls rub bear fat into their hair
till it shines in the sun like water, their young breasts,
swelling out, tilt more sharply, tender nipples
darkened and tight with blood. The first warm evening
Grandfather sits and croons to his chickadee
whose cap has gone gray, while Mother shakes her head
and glances at Father sideways. The merciless young
bicker and whine at bedtime, then sneak out
to probe the pond for frogs, the shadows for lovers,
while the not-quite-grown lie aching or stroke their way
halfway to the stars on single, shuddering wings.

One morning, lifeless all winter, the pond explodes!

APRIL 11

When, swollen with desire, I drop my robe
and strut before her, gut sucked flat as a drum,
cocking one eyebrow, singing a passion song
as if I were the Great Spirit himself
courting Mother Earth...

                      and she, my sweet thorn-flower,
my sugar-arrow, her lovely face downturned,
tucks her small feet more neatly under her thighs,
fixes a flawless braid, untwining, twining,
goes on sorting beads, or slicing meat for stew
as if I were not there...

           so that I droop
and, turning, slink about like a skunked dog,
a raccoon caught in the rain, a shapeless scrap
of shell unfit for ankle, wrist or neck,
and brush the dust from my robe...

                      until she sighs,
and, laughing, lifts the shadows from her eyes
that say, "All right, you idiot man, come on!"
and opens to me...

          O then I rise in glory
like sun at morning, streaming everywhere,
warming her hills and meadows in a flood
of radiance, brimming, bursting...

                   Afterwards,
lying so quiet we can hear the leaves
uncurling above us, it seems to me our love
is a perfect blossom floating endlessly
on shell-smooth water, and I can't imagine
how it could ever be otherwise with us...

as sometimes, when I'm boastful, or forget
to do something I'd promised, or let slip
some thoughtless phrase that wounds or rouses her
to anger or contempt, and all my words
of excuse or explanation are like salmon
rising to torchlight and the flash of spears.

APRIL 14

Greetings, pale one, you who came to our village
yesterday, uninvited, out of the blue
with one who speaks both our tongues, to hold a council,
and ate our stew and eyed our children's bare bodies
with wrinkled brow — you who had wrapped yourself
in layers of black despite the balmy day
and wiped sweat from your forehead constantly—
and looked upon our women's sun-bronzed breasts
with something more than shock or disapproval,
and when I sang one of our ancient spring songs,
in which Father Sky makes love to Mother Earth,
to honor and entertain you, squirmed as if
you'd sat on a swarming ant hill. You who brought
the thing you call a book, black as your robe
and filled with thin, dead, worm-infested leaves
you said contain the silent words of God,
who is a spirit greater than any of ours
like Long Nose or Stony Coat, or she whose breasts are
  blossoms,
greater, even, than the Great Spirit himself,
and the only spirit, all powerful, who created
everything, and causes all things to happen
and loves all people, even us who don't know him,
but is jealous of our spirits which we must give up,
and wants us to do this and not do that,
work hard all day and cover our women and children,
and if we do as he wishes will reward us
by sending us somewhere beyond the clouds called Heaven
when we die, where we will be nice and smile all day
forever, even though our mouths start to ache,
but if we disobey him will punish us
with sickness, maybe (and it's true we've heard
of other villages visited by white men
that were wiped out soon afterwards by disease)
and when we die throw us into a pit of flames
called Hell to roast forever but never cook;

and that what this God wanted us to do
right then and there was to get down on our knees
and hold the book in our hands and bend our heads
to kiss its blackness while you placed your hands
on our heads, one by one, and mumbled words
that made no sense to us — and so we did,
out of politeness and custom not to offend
a guest in our village, and also as a precaution
just in case all the things you said were true,
and out of respect for the magic thunder stick
you carried slung on your shoulder, which we have heard
is more powerful than a hundred arrows or spears
and has killed more than one brave who quarreled with white
   men.

We have discussed these matters most of the night
in our village council, and I, Bluefisher, was sent
to greet you, White Brother, and give you our best thoughts.
What good is this God of yours if you can't skin him
and cut him up for a stew and wear his coat,
or tremble at his great beauty, or plant his seed
to grow succotash, or put on his ugly face
to make the children behave or laugh at his pranks?
And if your God is so all powerful
and loves us, as you say, why did he allow
Death to come up through the underground wigwam's smoke
   hole?
and why does he let sickness kill innocent babies?
and evil men triumph in battle over good ones?
No, pale one, we prefer to keep our spirits
who seem more real and make more sense to us;
and if sickness spreads through our village, as it has
before, I will fast and chant and dance and pray
till the angered spirit who caused it is satisfied
and leaves us alone. You keep your one God — here
I've brought back your book — we'd rather kiss each other
than its cold blackness — when I felt your hands,
pale, veined with darkness, pressing down on my head

a chill ran through me, and I had a vision
that I was sinking slowly into a pit
cradled by some dark spirit — the Spirit of Death!

APRIL 18

In my dream I heard a voice out of the sky
calling me to arise. I spread my arms
and flew high, very high, past many clouds
until I saw a huge bird hovering
its vast wings stretching, cloudy white and blue,
clear across the sky. It called me, "Bluefisher,
why do you sit and sing when there are wolves
gathering in the woods, their snowy coats
bristling, their black jaws drooling, frothed with red?"
"I didn't know," I said. "Great Spirit, help me.
Tell me what I must do to save my people."
The voice said nothing further, but I saw
the great wings shrink till they became a man
who ran away singing, leading a band of people
across the sky, pursued by many wolves
howling and leaping at them; their snapping jaws
were black books dripping worms. As the people ran
they were dropping seeds of beans and corn, and I
ran after them, catching the seeds. The people vanished
and I flew down to earth to find the wigwams
around Earth Mother's Basket gone. I knelt
and wept for my people, beating my fists on the ground,
then felt the seeds I had caught. I opened my hands
and there were Running Deer, Goldwing, Little Squirrel
and all my people, looking up at me,
dancing and singing. This is what they sang:
"Remember the Massachusetts, we who sleep.
Remember the Massachusetts, planted deep."
So I got a sharp stick and dug many holes
all around the pond and planted my seed-people there.
And then I woke and found it was a dream,
but whether power dream or prophecy
I can't say, and I don't know what to do.

APRIL 20

Drummer of thunder, hurler of lightning, hear
O hear the prayers of my people. It has rained
off and on almost every day this spring
so that we've sat inside, the old ones grumbling
about their aches and pains, the children bored
and at each other's throats. This morning Goldwing,
usually so mild and patient, slapped Little Squirrel
for teasing Running Deer, and later on
threw me out of the wigwam when I crept up
behind her as she was sweeping and threw my arms
around her waist and squeezed her. Enough, moist spirit
of soggy robes and drizzle. Though we pray
for you to come to us in times of drought,
you've gone too far — if you keep up like this
you'll rot the beans and corn we're about to plant —
even the fish in the pond have started complaining
that the water tastes too thin with all this rain!
Some say it is the white man's gloomy God
who has darkened the sky this spring, but I don't believe it.
I think you're just working too hard, and need a break.
Why don't you suck in your breath and draw up the fog
that hangs over Earth Mother's Basket like a cloak
and take a few days vacation, somewhere to the south
(but not too far, as we'll need you soon again)
and give brother Sun his turn to come out and play?

APRIL 22

A day like the first day: sparkling, flawless, fresh
from the Great Spirit's fingers, just before
he set the world in motion. Blue so deep
it takes you to where beginning and end join hands
forever. Blossoming boughs hang breathlessly
like falls of frozen foam. Awash in light,
you feel as if you could do anything
you chose, but what you choose is to do nothing
but bloom in quiet warmth and sunlit wonder
while songbirds, waking, drowsily rehearse
their notes of joy and grief, and far above
silver wings hover, held by threads so fine
you can barely feel them snap as the creator,
drawing back, speaks the hushed command: "Begin!"

APRIL 24

Hear us, O Hobbamock, and spare your people.

Spirit of greatest evil — famine, drought, flood,
fire, pestilence — it's been many years
since I called to you, dancing in moonlight around the fire,
shaking my rattle, yelling, twisting and writhing,
singing, praying and chanting, while my people
sing with me, throwing their beads and moccasins,
the new clothes they've worked on all winter, cutting and
    sewing,
into the blazing flames as offerings
to your great powers, begging you to relent.

Hear us, O Hobbamock, and spare your people.

Spirit whose touch is agony, hear me now
as I fall down and moan and cover myself with ashes.
Forgive us for what we've done to anger you.
Was it our bowing to the white man's God
who mumbles from that black book? We have cast him out
and will not let him into our village again.

Hear us, O Hobbamock, and spare your people.

Whatever our foolish deeds, we pray, we beg you:
accept these many gifts and take away
this new disease that is spreading through the village
like fire through the woods in early autumn.
Already, just two days since the first small sparks,
many are sick and some are clearly dying,
burning up, covered with dark red streaks and blotches,
pus breaking out all over their bodies and faces,
and none of my roots or herbs or healing songs help.

Hear us, O Hobbamock, and spare your people.

Hobbamock, we are dust if you say, "Die!"
Flowers blooming in sunlight if you say, "Live!"
O let us live so that we can honor you
for as long as leaves sprout green in spring, and turn
gold and scarlet in autumn. Take away
this terrible sickness from our beloved grandmothers
and grandfathers who deserve to die in peace.
Lift the flames of your fingers from our small children
who have barely begun their lives — spare Trickling Water
and Squirming Trout, Slow Turtle, and Cooing Dove,
whose tiny hands can have done nothing to offend you,
and yet who can't eat or sleep now, screaming and screaming…

Hear us, O Hobbamock, and spare your people.

APRIL 25

The sky tonight is like a frosty web,
the moon a spider. Fly, my little dove,
to where sweet peace awaits you. Let my drum
steady your softly beating spirit wings.

Here for a season, you will never see
how blossoms fall before the fruits are ripe;
how fruits give way to a brief blaze of leaves
then bare sticks shaking in the bitter wind.

Forgive our tears at parting. Death, who takes
our loved ones from us, gives them back to keep
planted inside us, blooming quietly
as stars at evening. Rise now, turn away

and fly, fly onward, gladly; look ahead
to where a crowd, dear Grandmother among them,
is waiting to welcome you. Look, there she is
waving and smiling. That's it. Faster! Fly!

We won't be far behind you. Fly! Fly! Fly!

APRIL 28

I have fasted four days and stayed awake four nights
chanting and smoking the pipe with the eagle feather
whose rising plumes make a bridge between earth and sky,
awaiting a power vision, some sign to show me
a way to save my people. Nothing came.
Nothing. No voice, no image, from the sky.
Nothing. While my people are dying around me.

Great Spirit, have you abandoned the Massachusetts,
enraged at our kneeling to the white man's God?
Or has that pale spirit triumphed over you?
Forgive my suggesting it, but a shaman speaks truth,
or what he knows of truth, or his words are worthless.

Is it possible that this God, who scowls from the sky
at the loveliness of the body he created,
this God, who never laughs or thinks up tricks
to amuse his people, this scolding, jealous God
who's so greedy he wants to be the only one
and have everybody kneel down and worship him
and be serious, working from dawn to dusk every day,
and never tell dirty jokes…is it possible
that this passionless spirit's more powerful than you?

Great Spirit, if all the pale one said was true,
and that is why so many are sick and dying,
I think my people would rather die than serve
such a joyless spirit who has no lips to kiss
or arms to hug or sex to offer as gift
over and over again to the beloved
as flowers unfolding or rain pouring down from the sky.

Great Spirit, rather than live the white man's way,
I think we'd prefer to try the skewers of Hell
where, as we sizzled and dripped through eternity,

at least we'd be free of that maddening drone of advice
and could admire each other's nakedness.

APRIL 30

It is the same in every village now:
the Massachusetts are dying. I've put away
my rattle and drum, my herbs. The Massachusetts
are dying. Running Deer and Little Squirrel
buried yesterday. The Massachusetts are dying.
Everywhere packing and burning. The Massachusetts
are dying. Tomorrow what's left of the village will go.
The Massachusetts are dying. Goldwing is burning,
her body stinking with pus. The Massachusetts
are dying. I, too, am dying; there is blood
and shit on my bearskin. The Massachusetts are dying.
There will be no planting of beans and corn this year.
The Massachusetts are dying. My people instead
are being planted, as in the prophecy
of the dream I had. The Massachusetts are dying.
Farewell, Earth Mother's Basket. Your fish must fill
other people's bellies. The Massachusetts are dying.
May the pale ones, if they come to live by your banks,
learn to love and respect your animals, birds, trees, fish
and flowers, as we did. The Massachusetts are dying.
May they swim in your waters and run around your edge.
The Massachusetts are dying. And years from now
some other singer celebrate your beauty.
The Massachusetts are dying. And think of me
long ago, weaving my stories, chants, legends and songs.
The Massachusetts are dying. So that my people
like seeds in spring will poke up their sleepy heads
and blossom again. The Massachusetts are dying.

MAY 2

Farewell, Bluefisher. May your crumbling bones
some three hundred and fifty years ago
have fed the soil that fed the worm that slipped
from the hook to feed the fish that was caught by the gray-blue
great, great, ever-so-great grandfather
of the bird that inspired me to imagine you.

And may what I've written about you and your people,
though largely invention and most likely wrong
in many particulars, be true in spirit,
fact and imagination intertwining
as corn and beans growing together, the delicate vines
winding their blossoms around the sturdier stalks.

And may the reach and grandeur of your vision,
the flash of your wit, your insight's plunge and shock,
inspire me to make light of my bodily ills,
anxieties and frustrations, and breathe more deeply
as I circle Earth Mother's Basket, lifting my head
from brooding upon this self-destructive age
to rise up and gaze with you all ways at once
until I can feel the passionate dancing of atoms
in flowers and stars, vast galaxies spreading their petals,
and glimpse, in awe and wonder, the great design,
the brother-and-sisterhood of all creation
in which there are no strangers or enemies,
just creatures, linked in one cosmic family,
caught up together, whirling through space and time.

And may the spirit of the first Massachusetts,
reverent, joyous, springing up again
to live in these poems, tempt my people to dream
of a common wealth that has less to do with profits
than living in peace on a globe where nobody's starving,
honoring Mother Earth with love and respect —

instead of choking, stripping, mass-raping her
and leaving her to die, as we seem to be doing —
celebrating her rhythms of sun and rain,
seeding and harvesting, bud and blossom and fruit,
while the Great Spirit hovers over all
rejoicing in the variousness of his children:
fur, skin, bark, scale, feather; laughing features
of red and yellow, brown and black and white —
a dream that seems flickering, fading, ever-receding,
that could save us, still, if we'd let it; a dream than once
was true, or truer, and isn't over yet.

from

SOME SENSE OF TRANSCENDENCE

1999

MIDDLE AGE

Having somehow survived the traumas
of growing up, passing
from school into the world
of your first job, marriage, divorce, analysis
second marriage, suburbs, mortgage
womb terrors, deliveries, diapers
playgroups, Miss Von Krump at Nursery School

you arrive at an afternoon
when for the first time since what seems like forever
they've all disappeared, leaving you
on your own, for the moment,
one somewhere off at a schoolmate's
the other up the street, and your wife working late

and after you've relished the quiet luxury
of having nothing immediate to do
spreading out around you for half-an-hour
you find that you're really not quite sure what to do
with yourself, and you suddenly picture your mother
when you'd get home from dances, sitting up alone
on the porch in darkness, her cigarette flaring, dying

so you shake yourself and go down
to the basement to dust off the piano
but the notes have gone stiff and sour
so you come back up
and take down some Dostoyevsky
you haven't looked at since college
but it's underlined, with notes
in your first wife's hand
so you put on an old favorite Beethoven sonata
but it's fuzzy and scratched and repeats
and repeats and repeats
and by now you're in no mood

to attack that set of exams
you should have done over the weekend
or tangle with the new poem
that seemed hopelessly snarled this morning

and so, for the moment, defeated, you just sit still
at a loss, alone, in the living room, drowning in silence
a bit scared, resentful, and sorry for yourself
because here you are, after all those years
of responsible adulthood, having made it through
in one piece, if not exactly with flying colors
to middle age, and suddenly free at last
and nobody's handing out stars, or calling up
to ask if you can come out after dinner to play.

OLD WINE
(for Dorrit)

You could have gone
sharp and sour, thinned
by loss after loss after loss,
alone in some dim
room full of musty
furniture, nodding off, dreaming
of distant, sunlit
hillsides, young laughter, strong arms
pulling you down...

instead you kept growing
deeper, more varied, open
to light and dark,
giving yourself
in rich sips and swigs away,
letting grief, as it aged you,
bring out the subtle
bouquet of all you had been
as daughter, wife, mother — precious
balm to the world.

TRIPTYCH

1

Passing On
(for Dad)

For a time

I couldn't see
a gull sweep down to break
the skin of a pond

or hear Fats or Garner
growling over the keys,
their fingers scattering reckless
fistfulls of notes

or recall
the last time I saw you
at 5 a.m. in the driveway of the shore cottage
as we pulled out:
hands flapping, jumping up and down
in your weathered khakis, mud-caked basketball sneakers,
beard waggling, making faces at the kids —
the "eminent naturalist," still a kid yourself
four months before cancer dragged you down
again, for the final time…

without some sting or ache
as of violation
brimming my throat and eyes,
as if you had been torn
from things you loved,
or your loss had somehow knocked them
out of focus,
their contours blurring, smudged

by death's rough thumb.

Now, more and more
white wings curve
immaculate
against blue

strewn notes flow clear
in lusty
joyfulness

my bearded, scrunched-up mug
wags at my kids

as you settle back in
to all you used to be
and, sharing, gave me to treasure,
become, pass on.

2

Bonds
(for Mother)

Unlikely candidate
for a husband's pyre,
you fell, cracking six ribs
within a month of Dad's death,
and a few weeks later,
before we'd had time
to catch our breaths again,
were lying beside him, ashes
in the earth.

Loving parties as he loved nature and solitude,
bright queen of many a brilliant soiree,

witty and venomous,
with no focus to fulfill or make you happy
beyond such occasions
and wife and motherhood,
you lashed at him night after night
for fifty years,
yet never divorced
remarking, when you learned he had killed himself
after a nightmare year of pain and drugs,
"I'm glad for Brooke. I hope
he left half the pills." –
unable to believe, in those next few weeks
that he wasn't about
to knock at the door of your room
to take you to dinner.

And he, long-suffering
infuriatingly placid
saint that he was —
who could keep your sophisticated friends enthralled
for hours, detailing the sexlife of the earthworm —
confessed to me once, over twenty years ago,
driving me to the station after a visit,
when I dared to ask how he'd stood it all those years,
that he'd never stopped loving you.

In the motel parking lot,
the day before what was left of you was lowered
in a little fragrant sandalwood box you loved,
I heard a sudden commotion overhead
and, looking up, saw a couple
of Canada geese in tandem —
he leading, she close behind —
honking and stroking slowly across the sky.
They made me think, aside from the obvious
parallel to your deaths,
of the poem you stunned us by quoting

six weeks before, as we drove to bury Dad,
by the ancient Greek lyric poet, Callimachus,
in which he mourns the loss of a dear friend
with whom he'd so often "talked the sun down the sky."

Funny what you don't know
about people, lives.

It was Mike, the non-verbal one, supposedly,
of us three "kids,"
who stood up during the joint memorial service
and spoke so movingly
about how, despite everything
the two of you'd stuck together
through thick and thin

like those geese, I suppose,
who Val told us
bond for life.

And now you've gone to join him
in death as well,
releasing us from your anguish
into our lives
where we must learn to stop trying
to make you happy
who can never stop loving you.

3

Post-Mortem
(for Val and Mike)

you go on
with the rest of your life

plunging back into work
conversing
fixing breakfast
shopping for groceries
courting the angel of sleep

surprised by how easy it is —
between moments of wavering landscapes,
lava scalding your throat —
to cope

impressed by how far you've managed
to come on your own
and are likely to continue
before it's your turn to follow

resolving
to savor each day
as precious, miraculous
failing

picking up gestures, phrases,
the arc of a smile,
and other fragments
of immortality
that glint out at you
from memories, photos, the telephone
mirrors, your kids

probing gently, pearling over
with regret
the lodged, indissoluble grit
of awful times

a bit numbed
as if some secret organ or limb
had been cut out, or gone to sleep
so that you find yourself missing

little familiar things:
verb tenses, your step:

saying "has always loved"
when "has" is no longer correct

climbing the stairs with the tray
of Saturday morning
newspaper, coffee, toast
without the juice

fumbling carkeys with mittens,
a bundle under one arm,
then suddenly down
on the hard, packed snow of the parking lot,
clutching your ribs, or an ankle, gingerly
checking what's left of the eggs.

ASCENT

Leaving the autoroute we start to climb
through green into deeper green, winding up and around
rockface, the air, sweet with meadow, fresh with pine,
like the touch of someone who knows us well and loves us
despite everything, cool at our brows, gently wiping away
the film and grit of daily aggravations,
ambitions, failures, guilts, anxieties.

Halfway, as we stop to look out at the patchwork quilt
of farmland and forest sloping to snow-capped peaks,
the air by now so steeped in fragrances
we don't so much breathe as sip it, savoring,
a hidden bird close by begins to spill
such rapture, swelling, on and on, we shiver
feeling it pierce us, gather, rise and brim.

Arriving, toward nightfall, time seems to have skipped some
   beats
as the familiar red-cheeked, smiling matron
greets us, the same earth-brown farmers drinking beer
crowd round their table, the same rich cooking smells
follow us up the stairway to our room
whose beds are piled high with fairy toadstool puffs
onto which we collapse with sighs of utter bliss.

Waking, after dreamless sleep, to the sound
of water rushing, we open all the windows
and lie back naked, skin silked with early light,
your breasts echoing the mountains framed in the distance;
for a moment the sense that things have been like this
for a long, long time — forever maybe — broken
as I reach out to touch you, name you, and you turn.

Breakfast out on the terrace, sunlight caressing
everything, dancing, shimmering, iridescent
swallows feeding on air, geraniums

outblazing the raspberry, cherry, red currant jams
we scoop and spread with sweet butter over the pure
white inner nests of rolls, pouring cup after cup
from steaming pitchers of coffee and hot frothed milk.

Walking for hours along a grassy ridge,
dwarfed by encircling peaks, words fall away
as our spirits, soaring, merge with the primal grandeur
of rock and sky — creation, emptiness;
calling us back, at our feet, the sprinkled notes
of blue and gold bells and stars embellishing
an ever-stretching symphony of green.

Evening, exhausted, drunk with alpenglow,
wine and contentment, we stroll the quiet streets
of the village, gazing up at the scattered lights
of chalets in the high meadows, above them stars
in brightening patterns far beyond the scope
of Bear or Archer — infinite, bright hosts
locked endlessly in war or love with darkness.

Coming back down, next morning, slowly, in second,
one foot on the brake, into gas fumes, a thickening haze
of remembered schedules, deadlines, debts, we swear
this time it will be different — somehow we'll keep,
shining inside us, shedding soft radiance
on those around us, something of the eternal
mysterious, holy unity of things.

We have, after all, that perfect pebble we found
sparkling at us as we knelt to drink, somewhere
in one of our bags, and how could we forget
that sudden songburst flooding us, or the moment
we turned to each other, your opening lips like rose
and honey mingling — the same lips telling me now,
sharply, to shift into third and watch the road!

CRUCIFIXION
(attributed to Donatello, ca. 1450
San Piero a Sieve (Firenze)
Convento di Bosco ai Frati)

As opposed to the other
slim figures, heads drooping
sideways, limbs pinned, piteously
suspended, almost floating
upon the cross,
fresh trickles brightly streaking
the forehead, arms, and feet
of the noble, heroic
shell of the still unrisen
Son of God,

here hangs the naked body
of what, till a few minutes ago,
had been a skinny, short, plain-featured man,
vain of his close-cropped beard,
from whom the life has been drained slowly out —
the flesh not yet stinking,
dumbly straining, along with the bones,
to slump from the spikes
that skewer the no longer wriggling hands;
lids not quite closed over bulging orbs;
teeth clamped on the dry wafer
of the tongue;
chest and belly crosshatched
with clotted slits;
genitals shriveled;
one foot curled over the other,
the long toes splayed as if
in agony —

here hangs no chrysalis
but a dead man

in whom the spirit burned
to accomplish something
immense, profound, outrageous, radical
as turning hate and war to peace and love,
a spark that, flaming, caught, and, slowly, steadily,
ever more quickly widening, blazed and spread…

its bright source here
extinguished, openly, publicly
stamped out
by an alarmed, self-perpetuating world
which claims him now, waiting
to draw him down and back
to the dust from which
mysteriously, he rose.

PEACE MAKER
(for Daniel Berrigan)

Asked, for a change, to comment

not about pouring your blood
over nose cones, prisons, the Pentagon, Nicaragua
or other such obvious
places you'd recently been

but about what you thought
of Saint Francis of Assisi,

after what seemed an awkward
moment's shifting of gears;
dumbfoundment? bemusement? titters
rippling the crowd,

you mentioned a painting
given to you by an artist
dying of cancer

that portrayed the saint praying
one arm round his brother
wolf,
the latter looking ferocious
and none-too-well fed.

It made you wish
Saint Francis well,
you said,

and went on,
once the swell of uneasy amusement
at your cryptic understatement
had subsided,
to suggest that perhaps one measure

of a peace maker —
Gandhi, King, those
whose lives you have tried to live by —
is the tenacity
with which one is willing to bear
one's message, over and over,
down from some cherished mountain top
tower, porch, lectern,
and speak it
into the slobbering fangs of aggression

feeling the hot, sour breath
ablaze in your nostrils,
flinging an arm round the bony neck,
kneeling to pray

not just for the ravenous
creature panting beside you,
but that other, waiting
to gobble you up
inside.

BLUEBIRD FEATHER

dull gray
till you hold it up
turn it
to the light
slowly
so

SOME SENSE OF TRANSCENDENCE
(Mexico, 1987)

1

Everything tilts, is sinking
back to mud.

One aisle of the great Spanish cathedral
in Mexico City's Zocalo lists crazily
from the plumb lines of the long-corded chandeliers,
floor tiles cracking, spewed up — you lose your sense
of balance, order, the vast house of God
lurching back to the ancient marshy island
of Aztec Tenochtitlan. A stone's throw from there,
half-excavated, the colossal
pyramid-temples, drenched with centuries
of sacrifice, skewed also, plunge drunkenly back
through layer on layer of conquest, rebellion, dust
toward some obscure, fresh, primal flowering.

2

Second, guarded glances of surprise
darting up from brown, dark-eyed, wide-mouthed faces
as we stand squished in the Metro, or I shoulder my way
through the market near the Zocalo, clutching both zippers
of my backpack, robbed once already...but those looks
mingling curiosity with something hostile, suspicious,
and something of intrigue — almost as if
this light-skinned, whiskered figure might be
not just another rich, loud gringo tourist
but Cortes, Christ, or, even, this time, the true
Quetzalcoatl: wise, kind, gentle teacher,
plumed serpent, reconciler of opposites:
earth and air, light and darkness, flesh and spirit —

returned at last, as in the prophecy,
in his manifestation as a bearded white man,
to end a greedy, destructive, blood-drunk age
of savagery, and usher in some new
era of global peace and harmony.

And even as I smile at the idea
of this balding, middle-aged, junior-high teacher-poet,
with four remaindered slim volumes clogging my basement,
as conqueror or redeemer of *anything*,
I'm thinking: well, why not? Maybe it's not so crazy.
If a savior were to appear or return today,
why not as a shy, romantic, lyric poet
out of phase with his time, but heralding another
with the slighted strength of quiet empathy
for leaves and stars and the invisible
connecting forces that flow all around and within us?

3

beyond the tangible, evanescent
present, the catchy popular song
on the jukebox, the cherry Popsicle
on the steps of the museum, melting, fading
with cathedrals, pyramids, back to nothingness
in a seemingly godless world, without obvious purpose

some sense of transcendence, rising: mysterious
moments of wonder — sometimes the way the light
graces a cup, a mountain peak, lake, branch, shell,
or a face or a flower brushes you
with such beauty you feel yourself suddenly
welling, opening, flowing into some other
radiant, timeless unity…

4

Lord of Dawn, glimmering
Morning and Evening Star,
bridge between light and darkness,
is it you? Is it really you
who has risen out of the east
and come gliding over the sea on a floating hill
in this, the prophesied year of your return,
to claim again what was yours in ancient times?

O may it be so!
I, Moctezuma, ruler of Tenochtitlan,
emperor of all the land to both seas,
high priest of Huitzilopoctli, greedy Sun God —
preeminent in our times — but guardian still,
in my heart, of your quiet grace and modest wisdom,
pray it is you, Quetzalcoatl, come home at last
as I prepare to welcome
the tall, pale, bearded figure
approaching, a few minutes march
from the causeway to our city.

Creator of the sweet arts of civilization,
since your departure so long ago
the people have forgotten
your gentle ways, your selfless lessons
in how to elevate our sinful flesh,
the true, deep meaning of your sacrifice
when you cast yourself into the flames of a funeral pyre,
suffered torment in the underworld,
and rose again, purified, as the Morning Star.

What once was rich gesture, symbolic rite,
has turned into wholesale slaughter.
It is insane!

War in the name of religion,
religion war's insatiable prostitute!
Where, before, one honored volunteer
would mount, his heart aspiring higher and higher
with every step toward the waiting altar stone,
to give himself in ultimate sacrifice,
heart's blood returned to the sun who gives us life —
now thousands, taken in battle, are hauled up, bound,
screaming, chests slashed,
hearts ripped out, raised, still pulsing,
to the sky, then burned in the Sun God's honor,
heads and limbs hacked off, tossed
bouncing and slithering down the stinking stairs
blackened with rivers of blood.

O come now! It is time!
Feathered snake, balancing within yourself
the warring elements of flesh and spirit,
let your healing wings spread, rise, brightly hover
over this sick, dark age of humankind
so rich in gold and jewels, in pride and power,
but starved in spirit, compassion, true happiness.
We have marked the recent portents
of coming change:
the lake that surrounds our city suddenly
boiling, frothed with rage;
temples destroyed by lightning; the fiery comet
that rose and hung in the sky from midnight till dawn
like a flaming ear of corn.

But is it truly you
who even now I can see in the distance
like the head of some slowly uncoiling, monstrous serpent
as you ride along the causeway
leading your men on their strange, tall deer?
Let it be you, I pray, and not some foreign
gold-crazed adventurer or alien god

coming to smash our temples and build his own
with brick of our bones and blood.

I've listened with shock, misgiving,
growing terror,
to the rumors, reports
of the magical thunder sticks your warriors carry
slung on their shoulders
that have struck down our neighbors
who dared to oppose you,
and the iron clothing that I myself can see
gleaming in sunlight as your turn
and, laughing, shout to your men,
that seems so unlike you.

O gentle savior, how can it be you
who has returned,
for the great disks of fine-wrought gold and silver,
the neckbands of precious green feathers and gems,
the mirrors and crowns and other treasures I sent you,
this one rusty helmet,
battered, rank with sweat,
that I've filled with gold nuggets, at your command,
and hold now in trembling hands as I descend
and walk toward the city's opening gates to greet you?

5

from the fountained courtyard
of our Hotel de Cortes
the sound each morning of sweeping,
splashing, sweeping —
relentless, insistent
scrubbing at the crust
of centuries' grime

the parrot in its cage
clutching the rusty padlock
with one claw
and tonguing, tonguing the keyhole

the *Mexico City News,*
which we try to avoid,
headlining the sickness of the present
most powerful leader in the world;
his new cancer, chronic
unslakable thirst for arms

some rhythmic, metallic
pulsing from the city
that suddenly stops

the beautiful girl
in the Metro, nursing a baby
swaddled in her rebozo:
Madonna in sneakers and plaid skirt

the hole in the wall I found
off the market in Patzcuaro —
the only place open at 7 a.m. —
where two wrinkled women,
busy with bean stew in a huge frying pan,
welcome me, smiling,
day after day,
bringing a large, clear glass
of steaming milk, Nescafe, sugar,
as if to say, "Write,
write, write! Whatever it is,
it must be important."

6

the heart, then, welling, burning
to give itself
to some other, greater
urgency, design...

but to reconcile that
with its own dark thirst
for blood?

easy enough to imagine
the small self groping
beyond its meager bounds
to connect with some other
eager, trembling soul:
flinching, responding
blissfully twining, blending...

but to square that, here and now,
with the face turned away
on the pillow next to yours
in the ringing, widening darkness
after the rush of bitter words
that were finally loosed, and meant
and no gentle touch or pleading
can summon back?

the ache to envision some ideal
new age, dimly evolving
as, heart-in-heart, two-in-one,
we push on toward the obscure
realm of All-in-One
brushing the quick of others, feeling the shock
of difference, possibility,
asking shyly to learn, impatient to share
our local wisdoms, stories, names

for Jesus, Quetzalcoatl,
mingling, jostling, losing ourselves
going under, in darkness
furled, suspended, waiting

to rise again, somehow
lighter, more spacious, marveling
at the vast, spreading blossom
of the universe, glowing
all around and within us, flesh suffused
with joy, love, flickering, feathered
in soft light, poised
between night and morning: dawn…

but to catch any glimmering of that
at the block party, popping peanuts, guzzling beer
back to back with the guy whose succession of Dobermans
has scared the shit out of you and your kids
for the past twelve years;
and the woman whose manicured lawn
is your own mutt's favorite,
who glares from her window, quotes the local leash law,
and has sicked the cops on you a number of times;
the Santa Clausy senior citizen
whose business was candy
who waves and beams and sings out neighborly greetings
whenever you pass
and sets poisoned raccoon and squirrel traps
that did in one of your cats;
and the new, honey-blond young mother
whose succulent legs
you've nibbled on and up, as she suns in her yard,
but turns out to have zit pocks, hard, blank eyes,
and speaks with a whiny twang
about little but clothes?

7

the osprey I spotted
the other day, a month after we got back,
circling the nearby pond
where I stop for a minute, mornings
on my way out,
lucky to see a kingfisher or heron
along with the gulls and mallards
that still manage, somehow, to survive
the filthy water, rapidly silting in...

but, this time, majestic, silver-black, soaring wings
that, as I watched, folded, dropped
like a spear, spike, driven
by some unseen hammer, shattered
the calm, reflecting trees and sky,
kept going, pierced, plunged, disappeared
for what seemed more than seconds,
hours, light-years, the turbulence settling back
above it — so that I thought
it's knocked itself out, is drowning,
holding my breath—and then
came breaking through
again, the other way, struggling, wrestling
the heavy liquid pouring from it, spread
tremendous pinions and slapped, slammed, thrashed
the surface in a frenzy
of climbing, lunging forward, slowly rose
clutching, dragging something
bright, big, flashing
fiery gold in the sun —
too huge and wildly flailing, it seemed,
not to be dropped, escape —
but rowing, heaving, lifting, rose and rose,
then circled broadly, several times,
as if it too couldn't quite believe its catch

or to let the fisting needles
quiet that shuddering agony in its grasp,
and, finally, found a branch and settled there
for what must happen next...

As I drove off, heart-stunned, lost
in wonder, horror
still diving, wrenching up, gasping, slick with blood,
I suddenly thought: well, so much for transcendence!
then: no, wait — maybe that's how it *has* to be:
to plunge from some lofty vision
into the rich, stained beauty of the world,
feeling the dark swarm over our heads,
fierce nails drive through flesh and bone,
struggling up again, if at all,
body-and-spirit locked, inseparable:
dazzled, ecstatic, dying
as we ascend.

EMPTY NEST HAIKU

    Empty nest. Psych! Let's
gag the phone, strip, gaze, dance! You
    say, "Work. Fifties. No."

    You say, "I love you
but not like some roused goddess.
    That's how it is now."

    You say, "No one can
fulfill all another's needs."
    Our hearts cut like jewels?

    Strange season of new
passions in my middle years.
    You say, "Go and grow."

    Sax every night. New
York, half the week, exploring
    changes, loneliness.

    Amsterdam Ave. Glazed
dogshit. Heartache. Tip gigs. Still
    go for it happy.

    Each day three million
potential tantric lovers.
    Never so alone.

    All right all you tough
city slickers — where's someone
    with the guts to love?

    Friends say, "Blow your horn,
write. Be cool. Shaktis will come
    in butterfly swarms."

    Drawn by my open
sweet, compassionate vibe, they
       light, sip, rest, flit on.

    Warsaw…Osaka…
Newton…converge, join hands, dance
       in my bursting heart.

    You say, "You are free
to go, grow, fulfill yourself."
       They say, "You're married."

    Friend? Big brother? Saint?
or dirty old man, too weak
       to take more than thanks?

    Half empty, half full.
Tricks of perspective. Bullshit!
       Half anything sucks.

    MWM
seeks F open to explore
       unqualified love.

    Suppose I did find
a soul-and-body mate…where
       would home be Christmas?

    The urge to run home
hug you, safe, plead for a kind
       of love you don't feel.

    That book on tantric
ecstasy, flesh merged with soul —
       salvation or doom?

For you Earth's solid
foundation, labor, harvest.
   For me Heaven, Hell.

No sex without soul —
a resolve I shall live by.
   Your health, my left hand.

   If I did get in
some other's soul and pants, would
   the foundation crack?

Nirvana, please...but
new in-laws, mortgage, Huggies
   all over again?

So settle for art,
friends, ease back into comfy
   safe once-a-moon sex?

Gently, slowly, could
I wake the goddess in you?
   Or is she pure myth?

Checking back with you
about this one, that one, to see
   if you'll crack or flip.

Asking permission
of Mommy? Or consulting
   with an old true friend?

Infantile ache to
curl back into the womb? Or
   stretch out to the stars?

    Foundation. Base camp
from which to go exploring
    peaks shrouded in cloud.

    Terrified? You bet.
Poised, teetering dizzily
    at the crater's rim.

    Lava of desire
seething, shouldering up to
    connect with the sky.

    To enfold the new
without crushing the old — love's
    cramped "infinite pie"?

    Big Bang. Infinite
expansion, all ways at once.
    No point not center.

    Back, forth, back, forth, New
York, Boston, where am I from?
    Where am I going?

    The guts to accept
it all, contradictions, say
    here, this is me now.

    Each morning get up
stretch my bones, spirit, head out
    into the unknown.

    Each night exhausted,
goddess fantasies, rising,
    sinking down, down, down...

Keep open, moving.
To each new beauty, terror
   yes, keep saying yes!

Such wasted beauties
tell me such sorrowful things
   I start to hate men.

Shiva-Shakti? Shit!
For now talk, cappuccino,
   dance shy fingers, eyes.

Still, before I die
to connect, merge, let go, feel
   stars swarm in my cells.

I say, "I love you
but search for Shakti elsewhere.
   If I should find her…?"

SKIPPING SEX

"Let's skip sex,"
she says.
"It always gets so messy,
and I can tell it's already started
to cloud and sour and confuse
what has been such a beautiful
energy between us."

"Fine," I say —
"your choice.
As I've told you all along,
sex, for me,
is not what we're about
so much as the quiet
timeless, floating bliss
of being close
and feeling loved and safe."

"I can't decide about kissing,"
she says, after a while.

"I know," I say. "Kissing's tricky.
Maybe with lips clamped shut
would be OK?"

"I like that," she says.
"And hugging's allowed, but only
in a friendly sort of way."

"That's good," I say.
"Just like we're doing now."

"Exactly," she says.
"And gentle touching...confined
to...let's see...

head, and neck, and back…and arms."

"Sounds good to me," I say.

We lie there, skipping sex.

"But how," I wonder aloud
(after a timeless stretch
of friendly hugging
and a closed-mouth kiss or two)
"can I manage to dim the glow
that spreads like trickling honey
down into my belly
and the dark, fiery region
seething, just below
whenever we're holding hands?"

"I don't know," she says.

"It might be easier," I say,
"if you could avoid
those quick little jumpy squeezes
when our fingers are intertwined,
and those feathery circles
of deliciousness
you trace with satin tips
inside my palm."

"OK, I'll try
to remember that," she says.

"And when you laugh," I say,
"at some teasing idiocy of mine,
if you could just turn away
or use one hand to hide
that flash of ivory
and slithering pink,

I think I'd feel less lost
at the edge of some jungle
that scares me so, dares me
to enter and explore
until I drop and die."

"I see," she says.

"And those warm, pungent clouds
of seabreeze and rose and roots
that spice your breath
and snake up my nostrils
to attack my brain,
each puff a sweet, cruel death —
maybe a stick of spearmint gum
would help?"

"And your eyes," I continue,
breaking her wary silence —
"you could keep some shades
in a coat pocket…or here —
I'll get you a pair
of the ugliest ones I can find."

"Oh come on!" she laughs —
neglecting to turn, or hide
that prospect of savage lushness
that makes me collapse inside —
and gives me a playful slap.

"And when you call," I say,
stroking the sudden swarms
of blood invading my cheek,
"to give me my daily fix
of the various tints and flavors
trials and twists
your life's gone through

since we were last in touch,
or to detail, hour by hour,
your cluttered schedule
that makes it clearly impossible
to fit me in that day —
or when you're here, like this,
and tell me, for the third time,
you have to go,
I think it would ease
the unspoken tension significantly
if you could somehow, please —
if it's not beyond your choice —
remove those rustling silk ribbons
of mucus from your voice."

BUTTERFLY HAIKU

    The silk butterflies
you gave me have escaped. Soft
    knocking at my heart.

    The fear love won't come
again, wings sweeping the sky.
    The fear that it will.

    Then God caught a flake
of sunlight, added a drop
    of blood, and said, "Fly!"

    Across a stormy
sea of doubt, fear, confusion —
    hope's brave, foolish wings.

    Coffee. Your half smile
heavy. My kind, tired eyes.
    Sweet sips, wings resting.

    My hand lights on yours,
flits off, returns, settles.
    Yours opens: moist, dark, warm.

    From pain's chrysalis
wings stretching, so delicate
    Heaven would shred them.

    Sun. Air. Talk. Laughter.
Lids pulse, flutter. Suddenly
    trees shrink beneath us.

    Love spreads out one wing
of passion, one of friendship.
    Flying is balance.

ANGEL

A woman sits at the table next to mine
reading, alone, like me.
Two strangers, minding our own business,
resolved not to violate
what we sense are each other's
fragile, mending boundaries,
we are completely in love.

From the edge of one eye
I can see her head bent over her book
her face obscured by her arm
and cradling hand, one finger
winding tight, then letting slip
a lock of hair, over and over.

I do not turn when she looks up
to stare straight ahead
at what might have been,
drags on a cigarette, lifts her cold cup.

I know if I looked
the nose, too blunt or brittle,
the worn, chipped earshell,
the trace of an old scar
slicing the cheek,
or the overripe, bruised, or bitter
fruit of the mouth would confuse me.

I want her face to stay as it is now
flawless, so softly lit by grace
compassion, tenderness, desire, its revelation
would be too much to bear.

She does not look at me
for the same reason.

We are so happy
to have found each other at last
again, and this time
agreed not to meet,
not to let our eyes and voices
begin to explore one another
our bodies let go, embrace, with a deep moan
between agony and bliss, as our souls slide
through clothes and skin and terror
into each other,
acknowledging, with a ruby shiver
that we are going to be lovers,
that this, if the world keeps out of our way,
could be It.

We go on reading
letting the gentle shimmer
of the presence beside us
comfort and soothe and heal
our aching grief
for a vision dragged down in midflight
by the battered heart's failure
of faith and courage
over and over again

relieved to be holding each other
safely, at arm's length, eyes cast down,
two strangers in love completely
with the perfect being between us
resting its wings.

LITTLE DOUG
(poem on my fifty-fifth birthday)

"Mommy…Mommy…
Mommy…Daddy…
Mommy…"

A small, far voice
faint odor of paper-white
lilies, marzipan, salt…

"Mommy…Daddy…Mommy…
my eggs lake, the peeling
is ceiling monsters, a liger
at the bed of my edge, wings buzzbuzz
up my noses and ear…oh Dommy,
Maddy, the dark
too deep, moon poking
its lemon chickenfoot
hop, hop, hop, up my blanky, I'm all alone
drowning, drowning in jellystars…"

I press my ear
to the echoing shell inside me
and listen, breathing through cracks
the perfumed terror, fathomless aching
need.

The voice comes closer: "Don't leave me,
Mommy, the coats on hooks in the hall
are whispering scary things, the teacher
smells bony—where are you glowing? No, Mommy!
I want to go with you…don't o aglay!

"Mommy, the ocean won't stop
hissing and leaping and crashing, the Bandycramps
talk funny yahyah, spit clicks, laughing, swinging

me into the icy way graves, icy slicing
my legs and tummy, stabbing my eyes, laughing, laughing
and clissing, yahyah…Don't make me stay here, please,
Mommy,
come take me home.

"Curled tight on the top bunk I won't
fall awake if I stay off
moaning all night, Mr. Mad Flashlight
Eye says, 'Shut up and go to sleep, go to sleep,
so to gleep.' Curled tight I won't…every morning
in the mushy woods, whistling, cackling, I fall
behind, stumbling, my knees…owww! Daddy,
wormrogsnakeslime all over me,
blicking my lud, I know
you're ashamed of me, Maddy, but but
the others are shoulder, jigger, Dommy, I'm only
five fears old, oh please, please
let me hum comb…

"And Mommy, if Daddy's there, this time please
don't cry and moan,
dreaming at Scaddy, and Daddy don't
talk so soft, I can't—louder, tell Mommy
'I love you, Mommy, I love you,' and hold Mommy
tight in your arms, hug her, hugger, hugger
so close she can't woan and mail, and stroke her
pretty soft hair, gently, gently, and kiss her, I would
if I wasn't so little and flaking
under a lizard of spankies, oh Tummy
my mommy aches!

"Mommy, please stop now, listen,
yes, listen, remember
that sunny sweet summer
smell of hay in the barn, purply pigeons
cooing in honey-gold rafters, green fields and meadows

blossoming rubies and sapphires, sparkling cold streams
we splashed and shrieked in, stuck dragonflies
glistening in air, huge yellow and blue-green
tolloswales flittering off as we chased them
through jack-in-the-grasshoppers, tripped and fell splat
in the warm sweet long grass and lay laughing
and rolling together, crawling to look
for over a four-leaf clovers…cool lime
evenings, porch cots, fireflies, Mikey and me
farting and snorting till Daddy came out
and said, 'Enough now,' and sometimes, sometimes
sat down and made up a story, his Lucky Strike
fireflying in darkness: Tony Avocado
who lived in the bathtub drain and had such
magic adventures, then flew back
and shrank back down into the drain…
drifting off in the avocado-eyed hoohooing darkness…
fresh mornings of cream
and strawberry jammountains, all of us sitting together,
joking and plans and punny, you butter
go bacon a beach, eggsactly, the ponies just like in books only
smelling much stronger, the giant-wheeled tractor
jiggling and bumping us all the way
to heaven and back, pink cow balloons spurting
and foaming in silver buckets, and everything
flowing and shining, don't start again, Mommy,
I'll hug you, take care of you, Mommy, it's all right, oh
Dommy, Dommy, don't you remember that farm?"

CYCLE

Chipped slivers of light
slip all around me,
spin down to meet,
become their shadows.

Another harvest
of hopes and dreams
that greened and spread,
turning themselves to the sun,
drunk on sweet rain,
high on hot streams of gold,
flourished or failed,
drained now, exhausted, let go…

Another crop
of terrors, pains
straining to bear up
battered by gusts and storms
hanging on, twisted,
whirl now, curled, dizzily down…

till the ground is a maze
of scattered trash and treasure —
rose, ochre, scarlet,
topaz, garnet, mauve,
glad for release, rustling faintly, waiting
for frost's cold calm shield.

While naked trees
shiver skeletons, creak
and nod,
drifting into a blank
dream of endless rest,
muffled, snug in snow…

until the first
needles of green
prickle that numbness, pierce
and prod them from sleep
to stir, stretch
bleed and bloom
with anguish and joy, again.

A PURPLE ROSE
(for Pat)

No one before ever gave me
a purple rose
out of the blue
from the depths of night
to bathe my bleary eyes
at the bathroom mirror
with fresh delight
and spread that sweet
tingly feeling
from crown to toes
of how special I must be
just being me.

No one before
ever crinkled up her nose
smiling sunbeams at me
despite warnings of wrinkles
to let me know, over and over,
that I am the star
of her heart's favorite show.

No one before ever answered
my call to come out and play
in the green-gold meadows
of Wonder Childhood,
wandering, timeless
together through the Now
of beebells and clover
butterdreams, rainbow streams,
flopping to wallow
and whisper, with giggles and shrieks,
to the smiles of Father Sky and Mother Earth
in the warm fields of Yes.

No one before ever lay with me all morning
naked, belly to belly, mouth to mouth
without thinking it must be time
to turn away to more important things —
the news, piling bills, the phone,
brushing their shrill urgency aside
for some future Now,
stroking, soothing the marrow-ache
of a frightened child,
cries echoing through the dark
of half-a-century,
pouring her healing light
into that pit of terror, rage, and shame
that I labor each day, alone
to fill with self-fathering love
but cannot learn
to share, risk giving, receiving
despite fears of sudden emptiness or drowning
on my own.

No one before ever dared
to open and let me in
to the ghost-webbed, murky rooms
of old abandonments,
early, guilt-choked entanglements,
in caves where nightmares flutter
cling and swoop,
to let me touch the quick
and gently kiss and lick
that quivering, wounded core
of birthright pleasures.

No one before ever followed, on and on,
the snarled twists and turns
of hopes, doubts, visions, fears
that maze my head,
spinning out, interweaving

her own with mine
as we search for some glimmering
thread of Truth
to live by, extend, and grow,
while around our laced fingers, dreams
the sun climbs and sinks
behind porch, or bay, or leaves,
or the dark at the window softens
into dawn, and we laugh, groan, sleep.

No one before ever woke me
with tongue thrusting through my lips
or snailing my ear,
hands roaming, exploring, unashamed, everywhere,
rousing my sleepy desire
with wave after wave of tender
ecstasy sweeping my flesh
till I let go, in bliss, surrender,
or swelling, rise and shed
my pallid skin,
a green god emerging, turning
to greet his long-searched-for soul-mate
mother, sister, Earth goddess
blurred into one,
my cock-flute throbbing,
calling her into the ageless dance
of scepter and lotus,
breast chalice, sacred fount,
passion cresting and frothing
as we plunge and play
fins flashing, souls slipping in and out
of depths and currents, blue-green
ocean eyes.

No one before ever gave me
this feeling of being
so tremblingly alive,

at fifty-five growing,
delicate, vulnerable, bruised, newborn, exposed —
rich inner petals unfolding:
a purple rose.

WALLOWING

"Know what's funny?"

"What?"

"My knee hurts."

"Really?"

"Yep."

"Huh. And know what?"

"What?"

"Mine's stopped."

"Yeah, well…figures."

"Which one?"

We look from the pillow
at the snowy tangle
of knobs bulging the sheet.

"I can't tell," she says, laughing.

We give up, snuggling closer
letting slip all sense
of whose is which what.

VALENTINE
(for Pat, February 14, 1996)

Because we still refuse
to give up our right
to believe we deserve
to love and be loved,
be nurtured and nurture
heart, body, mind, and soul

despite the dim path ahead
bristling with childhood monsters
snarling, crouched to spring,
but lonely, perhaps, also, longing
for welcoming arms, forgiveness, gentle stroking,
to be set free to sprawl in sunlight
and go their ways
or pad along as our guides

and despite the deep pits behind us,
littered with rusty armor
shards of dreams,
we have crawled from, bleeding
fragile, slowly mending,
hoping our tears
will heal and keep the scars
of loss, rage, guilt, fear, sorrow
from closing us off for good,

we turn to each other
here and now
with hope and choice and courage
steadying our hands,
praying this time we will learn
to be strong enough to be tender,
brave enough to surrender
open to trust, let go

melting, giving, taking in
the miracle of each other,
as we plunge together
into the unknown
of each new day's
endless flux and flow.

EXPLORING
*(for Val, in memoriam
and Pat, in the now)*

1

We never found what we were looking for:
a stretch of leafy woods, a quiet
path we could explore
for an hour or two that late May afternoon
soaking in green, freshening with clear song
heads bleared and achy
from the drive half-way home across the state
after the morning's burial —
a walk before returning to the inn
to flop on the big bed, snuggle, flow with the lazy
late sunlight creeping across the ceiling and walls,
then wash up, come down for a relaxing drink
at the six-stooled Pub and Bar
and try to let go, ease down, and settle in
to a place we'd never been before.

The woods were guarded by **NO PARKING** signs,
the lakes by fences, dirt roads marked **BEWARE!**
visions of Eden blocked by glinting barrels
of local shotguns, pick-ups taking the curves
of narrow roads like bad-assed bats out of Hell.
We smiled, a bit tensely, said, "Well, we're exploring —"
having rejected the too-familiar spots
of candle-lit inns and well-marked trails
alive on weekends with peace-seeking city folk,
chipmunks, warblers, and ghosts of former times —
"and exploring's just that: you don't know what you'll find."
What we'd found was country, small towns geared for work,
privacy, weekend turkey hunts and fishing,
and that the curves and edges of our need
would not fit the puzzle of this posted landscape.

2

Giving up the walk, we pulled in at Travels End
that had the inviting look
of an old weathered tavern with some local tradition
in the village next to ours
with its gas station, pizza place, drug and general store —
but whatever it once was had been turned, inside
into a glossy, modern Italian restaurant,
the small bar crammed and nobody in a hurry.

We poked in at some neoned bar and grill
loud with TVs and blank-mouthed stares,
withdrew, and drove on to our inn
the guide book said was homey with nearby lakes.

3

Six-thirty when we arrived, tired and hungry,
we skipped our snuggle and laze
and had the mini pub-bar to ourselves,
sipping and taking in the local news
from the chatty owner and young waitresses
one of whose boyfriend had left a message
twenty minutes before, reporting some "small emergency"
involving their son — but when she'd called back
there'd been no answer. We offered our concern,
half-logical hopeful reassurances
to her jittery confusion, not daring to leave
in case he called from somewhere else
while she was on her way home.

Dewar's and Merlot seeping through the strain
of the day — my big sister's urn-globed ashes
sinking into a gouged dark cube of space
beneath a chiseled upright stone proclaiming

"And death shall have no dominion."
"Right!" I'd thought, chanting alien psalms and phrases
about sin and Hell and eternal resurrection,
still wobbly from the five-hour drive from Boston
the night before, through downpours, overtaking
hissing, red-eyed hundred-wheelers — with flashes of Val
from photos and dusty crevices in my brain:
introducing me, when I was in junior high
and she in college, to the riches of Hopkins and Thomas,
and encouraging my early fumbling attempts
at poetry; sitting side by side in chairs
in her dorm room, guiding me through the obscure logistics
of reaching across the darkened empty space
of a movie house to take a girl's sweaty hand
into one's clammy own —
while your sleepy, insistent sense,
gazing out at the streaming black,
that we were on some strange highway above clouds
floating below us over hidden valleys,
grew more and more surreal as fatigue set in,
and the thought of the family gathering next morning —
the sad, familiar faces, grave and bruised,
I'd somehow have to find words for
as we hugged and chatted, skimming
for an hour or two, our complex, uncertain lives —
seemed increasing beyond
what I, Welbutrin, and Ativan could handle.

4

Our dinner was an unexpected treat!
Wine and Scotch blunting the edges
of the day's anxieties, the unknowable future,
we eased and opened, talked about life and death,
despair and hope, the need people have for each other —
though they rarely dare to admit it —

life's weave of happiness, suffering…and a kind
of hazy, welling joy began to shimmer
as we communed and shared, became two blending
interconnected parts of the same being,
opening, exploring, on and on
a dense inner landscape of hidden hurts and fears
wanting to come out, be heard and understood
in the healing light of acceptance and compassion:
the clinging ghosts of our childhood dreads
of abandonment or engulfment; current forebodings,
in our fifties, of ending up unloved, alone;
the collapse of my marriage, after twenty-five years,
my leaving, the relief, the aftershock
of guilt and grief, rage, terror, disbelief,
the added stress of beginning to work through
complexities of the upcoming divorce;
your courageous vulnerability, prying open
defenses to take on, give yourself, again
to the potential nightmare
of another still-married man…

Alone together, able to speak it all out,
take in and feel for one another — no prophets,
but, in the midst of the unknown, committed
to nurturing what we had established
over a year of living mostly together,
getting used to each other's compulsions, frailties, quirks
we each feared would push the other's panic button,
and the latest wave of mingled joy, hope, fear
from my giving up my apartment
and moving in with you — the deepened sense
of acceptance, safety…the pangs of heightened risk.
Admitting it all, we held hands, smiled, and drank
to going for it, one day at a time,
doing our best to give love and support
to each other, whatever challenges might come up,
reaffirming our on-going mutual desire

for evolving, open, intimate, soul-body love.

5

We rose from the table different from when we'd sat,
tipped the waitress overgenerously, went out
into the glimmering evening, and found the walk
that had eluded us all afternoon
because of our too rigid image,
right by the inn: a wooden bridge, lilacs, a brook
swirling with new, winged life; then a little road
we climbed where a mother and kids were playing
with a soccer ball I rescued at one point
from disappearing downward into the dark.
We exchanged friendly greetings and strolled on,
hand-in-hand, checking out the half-lit houses,
looking down sideyards to the dusky lake,
feeling that we were family among family,
part of the whole global family, at risk,
all needing each other's love and nurturing;
and as I recalled the morning: tears and hugs
and heartfelt words and eyes brimmed with compassion,
I thought, well, maybe death really has no dominion
as each loving, kind, compassionate word or act
goes rippling on forever, coming out
again and again — as Val's encouraging help
was still at work in my poetry forty years later,
still nudging my hand to reach across dark space
and lace with yours, despite the risks, so glad
we'd found each other, were here together, pausing
to kiss or look at this and that — in no hurry
to get anywhere beyond the blissful moment
of where we were, here and now, gently linked together,
having found what we were really looking for
in a place we never would have thought to find it,
by just being, going on, through disappointment

at the fenced-off old, into the cloudy new,
not pushing, letting it be and evolve
in its own time, whatever way it would,
moving on, together, two separate, blended beings
at peace now, bathed in the quiet grace of love.

May, 1996

AN ORDINARY MORNING

You wake to the light
of an ordinary morning

but something about the way
it's reflecting, refracting, slightly
differently, as if reaching
into, beyond, the surfaces
of things more deeply, lovingly
reluctant to let them go…

and things themselves
(the warm, immaculate
sheet peeling back with your hand
to reveal a mysterious
castle at the edge of a darkly shining forest
in the midst of soft hills and valleys, honeyed plains
you recognize, but hardly knew were there)
more freshly aware, even reverently
what they always were, though blurring at the edges
and slipping in and out of each other's names
as at a party where everyone turns out
to be distantly related…

and suddenly, as you're pissing
a gold stream into an alabaster
chalice — you realize
that though it's the same old world
of heartbreak and politics, genocide, housework, pollution,
for the moment all that's been balanced,
panned back from, swept under
a fathomless surge of calm, grace, awe, love, joy…

and then, once you've squirmed back into your skin
and are strapping the day to your wrist
it hits you that you've arrived

at something that's beginning
to feel like a whole new way
of seeing things and being: a new age
of inextricably tangled fact and wonder
beautiful, terrible, beyond hope or despair,
that you must accept and try to celebrate
in its almost unbearable richness

though it seems to have little to do
with the quest you thought you were on
toward the solution to some definable problem,
and even as it begins may be nothing more
than a moment's frozen perspective
in which all that appears
to be constant, eternal, is really
heading off elsewhere, toward God knows what…
but by now you're up, dressed, ready
for almost anything.

from

ECHOES IN HEMLOCK GORGE
An American Sequence for the New Millennium

2003

HEMLOCK GORGE

an ageless, regenerating
cathedral of green
just off Route 9's
on-rushing motorized surf

where I walk most mornings,
after an early breakfast
at a diner that opens at 5,
through spring, summer, autumn
and winter, when I can

rich earth smells
of fecund decay and lush renewal,
leaf-carpeted paths
rain-freshened, or the sun's hand
like an old friend's
warm on my shoulders and neck

to the rock cliff
overlooking the upper dam
to gaze down at the falls,
its spray of milky foam
tinged a suspicious yellow,
and across to the long, low building
where a software start-up
has gutted the Mills Falls Restaurant
that flourished awhile in the shell
of the old silk mill
which sprang from the bones
of the long-standing saw and grist mills
that shot up soon after
the original dam, made of wood
first gagged the river in 1688

then along the ridge

and down a narrow gully
that leads to a pebbly beach
at a bend in the river
to gawk at Echo Bridge:
a massive, Roman-arched
granite aqueduct,
the second largest structure of its kind
in America in 1876
still toting its obsolete
empty iron pipes

then up a side path
to walk out onto the bridge
and, clutching my acrophobia,
glance down
upstream to the mill husk
shrunk to a picturesque toy
and downstream to where the river
throws its arms around Turtle Island,
plunges over the lower dam
and under Route 9

then back onto terra firma
to edge and slide my way
along a path that winds down
the steep bluff to the water
and stand on the bank and watch
for something — I'm not sure what —
signs, marvels, mysteries, gifts
from some unseen hand: the gray blur
of a kingfisher heading upstream;
a speckled hawk
in a high branch, majestically
surveying things far beyond me;
the sudden splash
of a fish, gone but for ripples
when I turn my head; a frog

nosing the surface, its slime-green eyes
checking me out; a pair
of moseying mallards nibbling
not ten feet from where I stand

then scrambling back up the bluff
to stroll, panting, along a broader trail
to Sitting Rock (as I call it),
just far enough off the path
to rest awhile, chill out
meditate and gaze
through dew-sparkling leaves
of emerald, topaz, ruby,
a chorus of nuthatches, chickadees
crows, bluejays, woodpeckers, mourning doves
calling me back
to the woods with its creek
down the hill from my childhood's house
where I can remember
the welling, magical sense
that something indescribably wonderful
was about to happen —
unaware that it already had:
just being there and feeling
caught up in the flow
of water and light
and leaf and wing and song —
a sense of cosmic belonging
still available, now
to me, and all of us
that we were in constant touch with
for millions of years,
and can be again
in five minutes, anytime
we pull off the highway
rest our machines and walk
(though, admittedly, if you're hanging

in the Big Apple,
or some other Mecca of Making It,
it may take a bit longer
on the subway or bus
to the concrete-collared park)
back into what has been here
for billions of years
and will be for billions more
once our species, with its gadgets
and physics and rage
for the ephemeral trinkets
of power, fame, fortune, success,
is moldering,
an insignificant speck
in the annuls of eternity
that God, the Great Spirit, Nature
or what you will
has wearied of, eons before,
having seen enough
of our history, civilizations,
so-called progress,
and moved on from
into some higher evolving state

then back to the parking lot,
chanting a final mantra
to the river and trees and sky
before strapping myself in
to the illusion of safety
and launching out into traffic
another day

MANTRA

whatever it is:
the latest rejection slip
with its printed checklist
of reasons they're returning
my unpostmodern, nonwastelandblindered work...

whatever's eating at me:
the relentless, roborazor
globe-scouring feeding frenzy
of sound-and-sight-bites
on the screen in the diner at breakfast
that rides an adrenaline rush
through scandal, disaster, violence, perversion
on a never-ending quest for higher ratings
and has little to do with news
that might be of import, healing perspective, to us
of those billions of unspectacular
acts of love and friendship, nurturing
compassion, sacrifice, restraint
commitment, creation, dream, sweat, compromise
at the core of humanity's
getting from day to day...

whatever the psychic sludge
of ego, disgust, frustration, angst, fatigue
that's polluting my being
as I edge my way along 60
watching my step, popping vitamins, aspirin
chain-chewing Nicorette
in hopes of arriving at 65, if not 90...

somehow, amazingly, morning after morning
a few paces along the path
from the parking lot into the woods
I can feel something start

to loosen, slip away
as the fresh scent of evergreen
oriole's liquid whistling, flicker or flash
of azure, scarlet, nodding pink-white cluster
invite my senses, and the hidden rush
of the falls swells to a roar as I approach
flowing into and through me with something I can't name
and have no need to as I stand and gaze
at the braided glossy strands of amber plunging
solid, constant, yet moving, never the same
from moment to moment, and, stretching, raise my arms
and eyes to the fireball blossoming low in the sky
or purple-and-crimson-splashed clouds, or whirling swarms
of tingly flakes, or raindrops rivuletting
the ridges, valleys, and forests of my face,
and chant my morning mantra:

> This flowing, miraculous
> universal whole
> deserves to be experienced
> perceived and celebrated
> with wonder, awe, and delight
>
> and so it shall be
> is being, right now
> by me.

RIVER

river
The Charles/Quinobequin

tirelessly
slithering, twisting, swirling
licking, nibbling, gnawing
rockface, ten thousand years
carving this gorge
since the last Ice Age, receding
blocked its old course to the sea

river
The Charles/Quinobequin

a foreign, long-dust-crowned king/
"river that turns on itself"

two clashing
concepts, attitudes
toward nature

the invaders casting
images of themselves
on the lithe, amber body:
dams and mills
to harness its power for profit
polluting, choking the pulse and flow
of shad, eel, alewife and salmon

the natives had netted in weirs
and splashed among, hauling
their catch up the bluff
to stewpot and drying wigwam, thriving
for millennia, respecting
the glistening, sinuous creature

as spirit, cousin, provider
and Other — attempting
to address its nature, ways
with a word: Quinobequin
that turns on itself

PEOPLE

It's rare I meet people
along these old woodland paths
so early in the morning
in our Cyber Age

so the ones I do
often seem special
somehow larger than life

most of them walking their dogs
as their reason or excuse
to get out into nature,
and they may well wonder
(as I frequently do myself)
what a lone soul like me
is up to out here by himself

though one other solitary
passed by me one morning
near Echo Bridge
then paused and called back to me
to smile, say good morning
and ask, as we came face to face
if I belonged to a church group —
wincing inside
with a sense of impending
hassle, violation
of my contemplative mood,
on a sudden impulse I spread
my arms to the lofty hemlocks
and replied, "*This* is my church!"
which seemed to impress
but not discourage him
from informing me
about his local band

of monotheistic believers
who gather to worship
at a site nearby
and encouraging me to come
join them some Sunday soon,
which I promised to think about
as I stepped away, turned
and proceeded down a green aisle
among my preferred
arboreal congregation...

One torrential morning last fall,
as I was on the verge
of the path that winds down to the river,
a large black dog
came bursting up from below
(out of Homer, *Beowulf*
Malory, Dante, Tolkien!)
and charged, snarling and bristling
to within a few inches
of where I stood frozen,
then, following him, a bobbing
ascending umbrella, shielding
as it turned out, the breath-taking features
of the most beautiful
blond young woman
who's ever ravished my gaze!

Torn between dealing
with her ferocious companion
and the dizzying prospect
of the approaching goddess,
I blurted, "It's all right! I like dogs."
to try to ease her concern
for my discomfort, standing there stuck
in my raincoat, Phillies cap
and deluge of terror and wonder

but she scarcely acknowledged my presence
and passed by, casually calling
her hellhound, who eventually
went trotting after her
though not without a few turns
and fierce warnings to me
not to even think about following.

Who *was* she?
Elf maiden? Dryad?
Artemis? Beatrice? Faerie Queene?
Woodwitch with her familiar?
I like to believe her
some modern incarnation
of an ageless Earth goddess,
Spirit of the Gorge,
evidence, prophetic sign
that, despite our globe-clutching
blood-and-sap-stained hands,
we lightskins can relearn
to live in sync with nature

and her dog was Nature itself
defending her mystic
integrity and bounds
from violation
by the likes of me

though, more probably, she was just
some local knockout fitness freak
on a pre-rush-hour power-walk,
equipped, with umbrella and Rottweiler
for any type
of elemental attack,
regarding me, furtively, as we passed
not as some mage, or lecherous
goat-shanked god of the woods,

but merely an old eccentric
potential molester…

And some guy — half black, I think,
a freckled tan —
young, handsome, sinewy, tall
not unfriendly, yet distant—
I've run into several times,
his dog the reverse of hers:
a slim, silky, long-haired mutt
who by now when she sees me
picks up her nosing pace
and comes loping
to nuzzle and wriggle and wag
as I praise and pat her
till her owner catches up
and nods with a faint smile
at our "How ya doin'?" "Good."
and they pass on.

So who's *he*?
symbol? mythic archetype?
maybe (why not?)
a contemporary young Arthur
or Parsifal — a fitting candidate,
fusing within himself
the light and the dark,
to slay the gold spider
that prowls the worldwideweb
and bind our spirit-starved
technofragmentation…

And who am I in all this?
What am I here for?
Where do I fit
in this echoing timeshaft
of returnity,

with my bald crown
chicken legs, grizzled beard?

No wounded Fisher King,
(I who hate seafood
and shied from leadership roles
throughout my teaching career),
but Merlin, perhaps,
still conjuring, hoping to guide
through the magic of poetry
some oblivious wasteland healer
toward his or her destiny;
or a kind of quester myself?
not Galahad, closer to Bors —
the one with the wife and kids,
too weathered, domesticated
for the fresh innocence
required to reach the Grail,
but who went along and returned
to bear witness
to the wonders he'd beheld

or none of the above?
just an aging, obscure
neotranscendental poet
who takes his pent-up
still-eager imagination
out for a daily ramble
in a small, still-unleveled slice
of suburban woods
as the new millennium dawns
in Hemlock Gorge.

OSPREY

Up on Echo Bridge one morning
I found an osprey
perched, at some distance
on a railing post.

I advanced slowly
in awe and wonder, thinking
he'll take off any second,
honored to be allowed
to approach this majestic, resting
lord of the sky

imagining he must have
some lofty message for me
from his lifelong perspective
overlooking things,
if I was worthy, wise enough
to receive it.

He didn't budge,
fixing me with a cold
imperious stare
as I came closer and closer,
until, at some point, I stopped,
concluding there must be something
ailing him
and mindful of his sharp beak
and razor talons.

I stood for a while
eyeball to eyeball with Nature,
then slowly backed off, turned
and came away
with his message concerning
this fisher king's toxic wasteland

and his question for all of us:
What's keeping Galahad?

STONE SPIRITS

I've often suspected I'm far from the first
person (nevermind less frantic creatures)
to settle and reflect
on Sitting Rock
since that last continental meltdown
prompted the river sculptor
to begin the gorge

and sometimes, as I'm sinking
through countless layers
of time and matter, piled underfoot
on my way to the molten
planetary core
for my daily infusion
of Earth Mother energy
and inspiration

I come upon other
earlier musing spirits
conjured from fantasy,
some books at the local library,
and who knows how many
other invisible threads
that compose the cosmic
skein of reality?

Ralph Waldo's one
whose spirit shell
I've slipped into and communed with
who, after a stint in Europe,
spent the summer of 1833
with his mother at a farmhouse
a half-hour's stroll from here
and wrote to a friend:
"These sleepy hollows,

full of savins and cinquefoil
seem to utter a quiet satire
at the ways of politics and man.
I think the robin and the finch
the only philosophers.
'Tis deep Sunday
in this woodcock's nest of ours
from one end of the week to the other."

which sounds pretty nice
and speaks to the same disaffection
with worldly affairs, and thirst
for nature's potent elixir
that draws me here mornings
nearly two centuries later,
but, at the same time, smacks
of the all-too-idyllic, myopic
(which I have to watch out for myself),
granted the bloodbath
that wiped out most
of a resident population
a hundred and fifty years earlier,
laying the ground
from which Emerson's tranquil vacation
and pastoral rhapsodizing
sprouted and bloomed...

and I doubt his words would have struck
a sympathetic chord
in his contemporary
millworker, toiling, six days a week
a few hundred yards upstream
who'd cross a small bridge
and climb the bluff at noon
to sit on the rock and munch
in glum, weary silence,
attempting to clear his head

of the ear-splitting screeching and grating
from 5 a.m. to 7 at night,
from which tortured labor he garnered
five bucks a week
and a church-punctured day of rest,
one of millions
of cogs in the great wheel
of industry, grinding out huge
fortunes for a few thousand
as it rolled across the land
of the free and the slave
and the home of the squaw and the brave
toward an ever-receding mirage
of democracy...

or the Sunday picnicker
from Boston, 50 years later
who came and sat on the rock
for an hour to escape
the cityfolk swarming the bank
around Echo Bridge, the latest
stampeding weekend craze,
each waiting his or her turn
to stand on the platform
under the great arch
and bellow the seemingly innocent
word: "July!"
whose second syllable
would be thrown back transfigured:
"Lie! Lie! Lie! Lie! Lie!"
up to seventeen times
to the cynical metropolitan
throng's delight,
and inspired one columnist
in a local paper
to report that there were "so many
and so distinctive repetitions

that all the neighboring wood
seemed to be filled with wild Indians,
rushing down from the hills
and with their terrible war-whoops
ready to dash into view
and annihilate all traces
of the surrounding civilization."

How's that for a fanciful
history-reconstructing
revelation
of our collective Caucasian
lingering fear and guilt
about what had really happened
hundreds of years before?

a time that was lived through
by another stone spirit
I've mused and marveled and mourned with:
Sits-on-a-Rock.

PRAYING INDIANS

Catherine Maugus
was the name inscribed
in the county register,
but Sits-on-a-Rock,
as her spirit was quick to inform me,
was what her own people called her
and how she regarded herself,
from her penchant since childhood
to sit a bit off from the others
and gaze and reflect and dream
and receive visions
she'd weave into poems and songs
that her village would take in
with wonder and delight.

Her father, John Maugus, swapped a gun
for two acres atop the bluff
and fishing rights below
in 1682
(six years before the first dam
was thrust through the lip
of the river's upper falls),
and Maugus, along with his mother,
and Sits-on-a-Rock and her husband,
Samuel "Praying Fox" Tray,
made camp and lived there
for many summers thereafter
as they had many summers before
the lightskins' strange concept
of land as property
started slicing up the region.

Right around here, where I settle
mornings, on Sitting Rock,
they set up their wigwams

for drying fish and sleeping,
gathered berries and nuts
herbs, roots and squash,
and tended their corn-and-bean field
after whose harvest they'd pack up
the fruits of their summer's labor
and with a few friends' assistance
return to their village
a day's walk from here.

The Mauguses and Sam Tray
belonged to the Natick branch
of Praying Indians,
so-called after the conversion
of their sachem, Waban,
by the Reverend John Eliot
to Christendom in 1634

though some of their Native handles —
Praying Fox, for example —
suggested more wily
survival adaptation
in the face of unswerving aggression
that soul-felt piety.

It was the Praying Indians
in 1675,
when serious fighting broke out
at the start of King Philip's War,
who declined to join
their heathen Native brothers
in their frantic attempt,
before it was too late,
to stamp out the white swarms'
fast-spreading, voracious invasion
of their traditional
hunting grounds, fishing streams

and sacred beliefs

and who, for their fidelity, refusal
to kill the transplanted brothers
they'd tried to accommodate
and live with in peace,
may have been richly rewarded
in Heaven, but not here on Earth,
as most of the Christian braves
were rounded up one night
without warning, shipped down the river
out into Boston Harbor,
and dumped on Deer Island
where they were confined
for the two-year war's duration,
living in wretched conditions
along with the deer
who'd swum there in herds to escape
the mainland wolves.

Starving, succumbing
to disease, exposure, despair,
thousands died on the island,
and those who survived
in sufficiently healthy shape
were shipped south and sold into slavery
at the war's end

which occurred when King Philip,
a k a Metacom, son
of Massasoit, the statued
still-cherished American hero,
who'd welcomed the battered band
of Mayflower questers,
sheltered and fed them, taught them the ways
of the northeastern woodland,
and guided them safely

through their first brutal winter
in what the uprooted, homesick
soon-to-be conquerors
would rename New England...

but, anyway, the war ended,
along with the dream
of sending the pale invaders
in tatters, hightailing it
back over the sea,
when this King Philip/Metacom
was finally killed and quartered
in 1676,
one of his severed hands
sent to an alderman
as a souvenir,
and his head hacked off
and jounced in a sack to Plymouth
where it was stuck on a pike,
paraded down Main Street, and posted
to be pecked at, rot, and grin
for a generation
at these victims of Old World
religious persecution
spreading God's Word in the New.

SITS-ON-A-ROCK

I make an arrow of my hands
sit back, eyes closed, and aim
for the womb of the Earth
breathing quietly, relaxing
every sinew, letting slip
all thought, hope, fear, joy, sorrow
as stone softens
and I feel myself start to sink
through layer on layer
of leaf, soil, root, and rock
down through vast darkness
plunging on and on
until I can feel the warmth
of her fertile throbbing
well, surge, and seep
into my feetroots, tingling up
ankles, calves, knees, and thighs
to flare into scarlet
flametongues lapping my loins
on into my belly's glistening
honeycomb
through evergreen sweetly
branching from my navel
up to the spreading rose
petals silking my breast
soon bathing the violet
songseeds aching
to burst from my throat
then up through my mouthcave
into the seajewel pulsing
my forehead, sweeping up
through my skull's clear crystal
to soar beyond hemlock
eagle, cloud, moon, sun
high as the hovering

starflocks spanning the sky
and skimming that silvery fire
draw it down
through my head and body
kindling every fiber
till it pours from my palms and arches
into the ground
and I sit breathing deeply and quiver
as wave after wave of luminous
colors stream through my being
vibrant, ecstatic
a rainbow flute connecting
Mother Earth and Father Sky
on which the Great Spirit is playing
the sacred song of creation's
orgasmic flow.

MEADOW

lying this luscious morning
in a nest of sweet shimmering
meadowgrass, little
buttercup and dandelion
suns sprinkled everywhere, glowing
green, crimson, violet fragrances
of flit, warble, graze, trickle, stirring
my senses, blurring
wing/petal, tendril/finger, heavy light
rainbowing eyebead and dewlash, soaking
my limbs in azure honey, languorous
Earth Mother sprawling brimmed
under Father Sky

GIFTS

"I'll give you the canoe
of the new moon
to glide in at night down the river
fishing for dreams.
What will you give me?"

"I'll give you the shining arrows
of the sun
to fill your quiver
when you go hunting for visions
among the clouds.
What will you give me?"

"I'll give you the stars
to hang around your neck
so that the flawless curves
of your breasts and lips
will glow with a soft light
as you walk in the village.
What will you give me?"

"I'll give you the rain
to glisten your cheeks and chest
and belly and thighs
so that my friends will curse me
for my good fortune.
What will you give me"

"I'll give you a handful of feathers
from dawnbird and sunsetbird
to flash in your lustrous braids
so that all can see
the glory and span of your spirit.
What will you give me?"

"I'll give you a pouch of flakes
from all the butterflies
to sprinkle in the black bristles
that arc your scalp
so that all will know
the brave whose spirit can weave
a rainbow out of a storm.
What will you give me?"

"I'll give you my flute
that, coaxed by your gentle fingers
soft mouth, warm breath
will play a sweet tune
of such exquisite desire
it will lift us to where the streams
of starlight and blood flow as one.
What will you give me?"

"I'll give you a magic sheath
to slip your flute in
that will bring it to life
and teach it to dance and play
a song of such passion and joy
new spirits will issue from it
to bring tender pride to your manhood
and comfort of our old age.
What will you give me?"

"I'll give you my love
and all that I am forever.
What will you give me?"

"I'll give you my love
and all that I am forever
and ask in return nothing more."

SITS-ON-A-COCK

"Sits-on-a-Cock!" he whispered —
shameless brave!
But oh, it was lovely
beyond anything
to lean back in his lap,
his arms around me, his hands
brushing flame from my skin,
and feel his manstalk inside me
swelling, shooting up and out
sweet sun-drenched petals of pleasure
that scattered, dissolved into luminous
waves sweeping up, then ebbing
to build again, higher and higher
through my chest and throat into my scalp
until I could feel my skull melting
my whole being start to collapse
around his warm throbbing as the first spurt
of seed gushed into my womb
and we crested, blurring, together
in ecstasy, plunging
to slam, break, burst, and go rushing
blindly, somewhere, on and on…
slowing at last, subsiding
to ease and eddy and end
in a cloud of glistening
tingly iridescence
on the shore of some quiet, timeless
island of bliss…
drawn back too soon
from the edge of sleep by a moon
that had leapt across the sky
and a far voice calling
"Come in, you two. It's late!"

STEWPOT

In my dream I saw a stewpot
much like ours, bubbling
with fish and vegetables and fragrant herbs,
but around the below the rim
were set seven sparkling stones
each of a different color
and each with a vision inside.

In the first stone I saw
two lovers making love
and through them one spirit
of circling fire streamed.
That stone was the bloodbird's color.

In the second I saw
two butterflies playfully
spiraling, dancing in air
who turned, as I watched
into leaves and went whirling away.
That stone was the sunbeam's color.

In the third I saw
two feet deeply rooted
in Mother Earth
and two arms stretching
into Father Sky.
That stone was the hemlock's color.

In the fourth I saw
a necklace of linked hands
arcing across the sky
from East to West
that crossed with another
arcing from North to South.
That stone was the rose heart's color.

In the fifth I saw
a throat dressed in gleaming feathers
swelling with song
till it burst into flames and flight.
That stone was the ripe grape's color.

In the sixth I saw
an eye that was dreaming
flutter and slowly open
into a nest of stars.
That stone was the clear sky's color.

In the seventh I saw
the endlessly changing, unchanging
ocean of all that is.
That stone was the iridescent
seafoam's colors.

Then the stewpot grew big as a hill
and I saw a ring of people
redskins and lightskins
and brown, black, and yellowskins
walking around the rim
in a sacred manner

and a voice rose out of the stewpot
and said, "Eat!
There is plenty for everyone.
Sit down together and take your fill.
It is good."

RETURN

He came back broken
drained, an empty shell
of the husband, father, brave
they'd snatched from us that night
two years before.

We learned from others
who still, with shaking
voices and hands, could speak
how it was on the island:
the cold, the hunger, the torture
of not knowing when
or how it was going to end,
then in spring warm breezes bearing
decay's stench everywhere,
and summer's thick boredom, shattered
by terror when lightskins, circling
in boats, pointing and laughing
would open fire for sport.

I'm convinced he still knows us — his eyes
always brighten when Dressed-in-Corn-Leaves
brings him a meal, or I
stroke his arm, telling him stories,
but what's strange is the smile
that lights his face most of the time
even when we forget
to bring him in from his tree
at the first drops of a shower,
or his loincloth's stinking with shit,
or the time I shrieked off a wolf
a leap away, sniffing at him.

Many call us lucky,
and I know what they mean

when I hear some of the others
through the long nights of winter
waking from dreams —

and he has his pleasures:
eating — his lean body's grown
sleek and round as a squash —
and staring at things for hours: clouds
as they build or dwindle and pass,
and birds and squirrels
moving about in the branches,
and the dog stretched at his side
waiting patiently
for his spirit to return...

so either he's not aware
or doesn't mind
what's become of him —
I sometimes think if he could
he'd tell us he's relieved
to be done with the lightskins
and watching the old ways die

and more and more often at night,
hearing the gurgles and sighs
from the bearskin alongside mine,
my loins ablaze, an unmelting
icearrow lodged in my gut,
I picture the two of us lying
in each other's arms, our bodies
blurring, mingling, blissfully
back into Mother Earth.

QUESTION

What dark, bitter, despairing
shriveled thing
comes to us sometimes
from gaps between sleep and waking
to question the meaning, purpose
of our lives, dreams, everything
in the swirling cosmos?

What answer could smooth
those pinched features, fill
the hollow ache, mend
that gouged heart, reassemble
such mazed shards of vision?

Better to not even try,
but just gather the slack bony sack,
cradle its acrid odor,
and stroke it, rocking and sighing,
"Yes, I know. Yes. Oh yes!"

until the light
drumbeat of rain on leaves,
or cry from beak or lips
startles the stalled flesh
into activity

and we rise to find
the sour creature vanished,
only a faint scent still clinging
as we begin the day's
necessities, here and there brightened
by a bud's breaking smile,
fin's flash, wing's flutter, familiar
hand's gesture, touch, beloved
slope of hillside or shoulder

with no answer
to the tucked, troubling question
except, perhaps, in moments
of earned rest, floating
quiet, the reflection
that there are choices,
urgencies, presented
that rouse in us feelings
of connection, being needed
and therefore important

and inklings of something beyond
despair or happiness
when the spirit expands
with heightened attention, swept
by a wave of wonder
at the privilege, gift, of being
here, aware, part of the vast
mysterious flow.

LOOK!

The light this morning
keeps saying, "Look!"
pointing to the green sheen
of moss rich and soft
as a deer's flank,
a fallen branch reaching
its spiderwebbed fingers
to scoop bugs swirling over the river,
the patch of sky tucked
in a brown wing gliding by,
leaping from darkness, the silvery
fins of a star…

until I can see the miraculous
whole of creation
where there's no death
but only transfiguration,
one thing lying down
to rise as another:
flake/flower, skull/pumpkin
endlessly interwoven
in a bright circling pattern
I never noticed before
the light started saying
so clearly, lovingly,
"Look! Look! Look!"

SAWMILL

This morning I heard the Grandfather
Hemlocks chanting in green
whispers among themselves
the long praising list of names
for all of creation:
sun, moon, star, wind,
rain, stream, rock…on and on
until they came to the last one
where there was much debate, confusion
how to name the thing
that bites through trunk and limb
while lapping the river and screaming
from dawn to dusk, day after day,
but never fills its belly.

"Monster," one ventured.
"Death!" exclaimed another.
"Time," tried a third.
But nothing seemed to fit
and they couldn't agree and settle.

"Sawmill," I offered, respectfully,
"is what the lightskins call it."
After a silence, "sawmill," one whispered.
Then another tasted it: "sawmill."
And they passed it around while
their heads faintly shaking and nodding,
but the juice had gone out of their tongues
and their hands were trembling.

DRESSED-IN-CORN-LEAVES

And now it's my raspy voice
calling them in,
a gray woman lying alone
in the dark with pain
threading my limbs and spirit.

How quickly things change
and cycle — I can still see
the little girl hopping
and stooping, naked
to butterflies and bees
along the tall corn and bean rows
as I weeded and watered,
snatches of song and banter
floating up on the breeze
from the men working the weir,

and when I looked up
she was dancing,
long leaves in both hands
at her waist, swirling around her.
"Dressed-in-Corn-Leaves!" I called,
and she came skipping and laughing
into my arms
and we hugged and laughed together,
for it is a joyful
as well as a sacred thing
when your true name comes
and the old dry mask slips away.

And that evening we performed
the green corn ceremony:
Grandmother, Father, Praying Fox
and me in a dancing circle
of which she was the center

whirling with pride and delight
in the leafskirt I'd woven for her

who now I call out to again,
whispering, giggling and sighing
with her brave on the rock, as the moon
crawls down the wigwam's skin.

SINKING CANOE

This chilly morning I noticed
a half-submerged lump of log
that made me think
of an overturned canoe,
in its decay still supporting
a tiny forest —
how beautiful the intricate
spray of green stems and leaves
still shooting up, swaying
their sunlit arms and faces
in praise to Father Sky,
and how sad to be rooted
in the rot of that sinking canoe —
like my people, I thought,
my gaze blurring as I turned
and climbed slowly, weeping
to sit and sway on my rock.

WHY NOT STAY?

Now the first finger bones
of trees quake in the wind.
Mornings I tuck my hands
in my armpits as I stand
and sip the river's dank breath,
then climb to my rock, thinking soon
we will take down the wigwams,
pack the smoked fish, squash, beans
herbs, berries and corn,
and return to the village.

It will be good
to catch up and gossip
with Outchatters Sparrows,
spice cider and lounge
by the fire with Drowsy Bear,
and weave dreams with Looks-Over-Mountains

but the thought of lying
each night more alone
as ice skins the water jars
often seems more than I can bear
any longer

and a voice whispers, "Why not stay
and sit here while the leaves
weave a beautiful blanket around you,
and quietly drift and dream
till the snowflakes have turned
your silver-streaked braids pure white?"

GYRE

This morning, shuffling along
the leaf-strewn path to the falls,
I could sense Sits-on-a-Rock
had gone back to her village,
leaving me to witness and mull,
three centuries later,
crabapples dulling
ruby to garnet to brown,
bees crawling groggily
in the ooze of burst berries,
and pale, bending, wind-tousled meadowgrass
ripe for release.

As I stood on the pebbly bank
for a windless moment the river
unwrinkling, echoed
the great arch of the bridge,
completing an endless round
of stone and water
action and reflection
nature, culture,
and my life's rich skein
of hopes and fears, dreams, joys and sorrows
was breathlessly caught up
with the green surge of spring and summer
autumn's bright blaze
and the long white sleep to come
in the sweep of the years' ceaseless gyre.

JANUARY

Now the dark, drowsy river
pulls up an icy sheet,
spreads out its flake-down comforter,
and, mumbling something
about swooping rocks and frogs
spitting silk and sawdust,
snuggles down into its bed
and dreams toward spring.

FEBRUARY

Day after day a stark
world of white, watching
for signs, sunny mornings the meadow
a shimmer as I raise my arms
and send forth my silvery mantra:
a gray hawk hunched in bare branches
over the frozen river;
a woodpecker thonking
life from a dead tree;
six geese arrowheading upstream
toward some distant source…
I stand listening hard to the silence
of sleeping seeds.

Still in the thick of winter
it's tricky getting out
just to the falls—pocked layers
of ice and snow on the path,
a glazed crust on the sides.
I stamp my boots searching
for firm foundation,
every step an adventure, risk
as with each new poem:
am I going to break through
to some deep-sunken chalice
of ageless, restorative wisdom,
or the shards of a fizzled
late-summer Bud-Light affair?

WHITE DUCK

This morning,
the first day of April, 2001,
as I stood shivering on the bank
for the second time since December
watching with awe and delight
the swirl and scud
of the frothy river, swollen
with snowmelt and recent rain,

a large white duck
such as I'd never seen here
among the occasional mallards
came shooting in midstream around the bend
like some spontaneous
infleshment of foam,
and, when it noticed me, turned
and beelined in my direction.
Here comes another message, I thought,
from the gods or the Great Spirit.
I hope I'm up to it!

The duck soon arrived
and came scrambling up out of the water
to frantically quack and bob
around my boots.
The first shock of bodily contact
shattered the mystic spell,
and, wary, but pretty sure
I wasn't about to be ravished
by some metamorphosed
foam-spawned Aphrodite,
my wonder turned into concern
for the poor creature
who might well be starving
right at my feet —

a cruel, pathetic example
of how we've treated nature
in recent centuries —
domesticating, transfiguring it
with the wand of science
for our commercial, self-absorbed purposes,
and then, when it no longer served them,
abandoning, tossing it back
to fend for itself
in the delicate web of the wild.

I told her I was so sorry
(thinking of it as a she
from my goddess association,
through the anthropo-engineered being's
immaculate white
could have signified either, or neither)...
so sorry, I said
that I didn't have any food
to offer her — then remembered
the half-consumed raspberry Danish
I'd stuffed in my jacket pocket
in a coffee house some days before
and forgotten about.
Sure enough, it was there.
So I tore off a few crumbling chunks
which, before I had time to drop them,
she gobbled ravenously
right out of my fingers
till I threw the remaining scraps
out into the water
to get her famished frenzy
away from me,
by which time a pair of mallards
had arrived, and managed to claim
a few flakes for themselves,

Then the three, concluding
I had nothing more for them
(as I stuffed the sticky wrapper
back into my pocket, and pulled on my gloves),
circled a few times,
poking at a deceptive
remnant of leaf,
and took off together,
the big white maintaining
a cautious, respectful distance
but seeming OK, accepted
as part of the natural
aquatic scene

which reassured me somewhat
about her half-tamed chances
for survival,
but also caused me to wonder,
as I stood there watching them go,
what we in the name of progress
have truly accomplished,
and to what point we lightskinned
April fools have arrived
on this chilly spring morning
of a new millennium,
and what's to become of us
and our darker sisters and brothers
as we paddle on uneasily
side by side.

WHITE SNEAKER

A tiny white sneaker, this morning,
propped on the ledge of the notice board
at the entrance to the gorge
brought to mind the legend
of the "Baby Ghost"
I read about last summer
in the 1889 *King's Handbook of Newton*:

a "wee spectre," it recounted,
that fifty years earlier
"credulous country folk
used to gather to watch for"
on the Elliot Street bridge
that still spans the river
at the edge of the parking lot —
a child of "mysterious origin"
who was believed
to float down the river at times
in a moonlit cradle that many said
could be heard quietly rocking
under the bridge.

Maybe its source was a Native
infant who succumbed
to one of the diseases spread
along with the word of God
by the lightskins when they arrived,
that ravaged the indigenous population —
the cold babe swaddled and set
afloat in a mini-canoe
to drift down the river
to the spirit world…

but I see it as the ghost
of the childlike wonder and joy

of life along the river
in a time when people and nature
were more closely interwoven,
an unbroken web —
a spectre whose bobbing spirit
is going to haunt us
till someone — perhaps the young shedder
of that small white shoe —
shucks the synthetic crust
of the last few centuries
and wades in to rescue it
from its river-rocked cradle
under the concrete bridge,
claims, nurtures, lovingly rears it
to lead us, like Moses,
to some dreamed-of land
of sweetly flowing global harmony

if enough credulous folk,
attentive to the whispers
of the invisible,
can be found in this proof-minded
materialistic age
to breathe life into that still
glimmering vision.

TWO INCIDENTS

Two incidents, this morning,
and some reflection.

The first in a thicket of brush
near the parking lot
where, as I approached,
a bushy red dog was frantically
barking and thrashing about,
while its owner waited, watching
from a ways up the path,
till a rabbit came spurting out
and bounded across the meadow —
the dog hot in pursuit —
toward Elliot Street
where it made a sharp right
plunged, with the dog, into traffic
and disappeared,
by which time the owner
was charging down the path screaming
"Eric! Eric! Eric!"
gasping out, as she passed me,
with some mix of guilt and defensiveness,
"This is a new one!"

The second some half-hour later
as I stood on the riverbank,
arms raised, chanting my mantra,
and a mallard swooshed by
and splashed down near Turtle Island
not far from where the white misfit
was puttering and moping
in the place where I've seen it most mornings
since I fed it my stale half-Danish
a couple of weeks ago,
alone, but, so far, surviving

in the wild
and never coming back
for another handout from me,
which I take as a hopeful sign
if no tribute to Peet's Danish —
but then the male mallard
began quacking and cruising along
toward his swan-like
half-domesticated cousin
who perked up, came waddling
to the water's edge, and plopped in,
and the two new buddies or lovers
went gliding off together
around the bend.

I hold these two incidents
up for contemplation
as crucial threads
in the complex present-day skein.

No doubt the long Native era
in what we've named America
was by no means a Paradise,
with creatures (humans included)
hunting other creatures,
killing and eating them
or being devoured —
but back then nobody had to deal,
while rustling up breakfast or dinner,
with running into a stream
of motorized traffic
where both prey and predator
could get instantly squished
for neither's benefit —
so this hazard's "a new one,"
as the dog's owner remarked,
that we've created and are responsible for

and could choose to stand back from
and consider carefully
whether it's getting us
where we want to go.

At the same time
the white duck and mallard pair
suggest to me that my vision
of us lightskins being helped
by another look
at our country's heritage
toward some more natural
healthy way of life
may be more than a wistful
over-the-shoulder glance
through nostalgia-tinged lenses,
and a real possibility
that I, in fact, witnessed this morning
evolving in microcosm
with my naked eyes.

RUN OF THE CHARLES

Having missed my morning amble
the past few days
when things got —
as my New York friends often put it —
totally crazy,
I arrived this morning to the shock
of a parking lot filled
with cars, milling people,
and a portable toilet stall,
the meadow sprouting
balloons and tables and chairs,
bright canoes lining the riverbank,
and the notice board crammed
with flyers advertising
the April 29, 2001
Run of the Charles
Canoe and Kayak Race.

"Join top paddlers," I read,
"from Canada and the United States
as well as amateurs
ages 12 to 80.

"As a Run of the Charles spectator
root on your favorite team
and enjoy the competition
from Dedham to the finish line
festivities at Herter Park."

Resisting my first, sharp impulse
to retreat and skip
the day's woodland stroll,
I decided to set off as usual
and see what I'd find —
these, after all, were not hostile

invaders from Mars,
bur fellow human beings,
and I liked the idea
that, for whatever purpose,
they were coming in contact
this morning with Hemlock Gorge.

The path to the falls
was marked as a portage route
strung with humorous signs
urging on flagging contestants —
no canoes or kayaks as yet
were bobbing along it,
just a few pairs and parties
checking it out
who quickly outdistanced or overtook
my moseying pace.

I swerved from the rock ledge
where I chant my mantra,
as someone was sprawled there
in the early sun,
and leaned on a railing
enjoying a sideview
of a wall of amber plunging
to shatter in creamy foam,
where I was joined by a couple
of soon-to-be racers,
one of whom said to the other,
"This is nothing!"

Two people were standing
on the bank at my first descent
so I bypassed that too and went on
hoping to soon encounter
a stretch of solitude.

A little girl and her parents
were up on Echo Bridge
and I walked out just far enough
to see more balloons
marking portage points below,
then gave up on the river
and headed for Sitting Rock
on the trail that no one so far
had thought to explore.

I can't recall if I tried
to meditate, or just sat
and gazed for awhile,
but I soon began to hear
shouts coming up from the river,
so I picked up my Phillies cap
and started back,
stopping to join the family
on the bridge, looking down
at the bright-jerseyed pairs of racers
lunging along the path
with their upside-down jouncing canoes,
flipping them into the water,
then leaping in and furiously
stabbing the river, yelling
commands to switch paddling sides
encouragements and rebukes
to their flailing partners
as they picked up speed and came shooting
under the bridge.

My initial fascination
with the novelty
of such bursts of excitement
breaking the quiet flow
of my accustomed routine
quickly lost its edge

as each new straining duo
began to seem cloned from the last,
and by now the girl
was starting to whine and fuss
and tug at her parents
having had, evidently, enough
of enjoying the competition.

So I left the bridge
and made my way back to the car
on a nearby street,
conceiving along the way
an alternative anti-race:
The Paddling & Portaging
Quinobequin Meditation
whose laurels would deck
the boat with the longest time
between start and finish,
the participants competing
for slowness and grace
of coupled step and stroke,
pairs striving to become one
with earth and water,
each passing wildflower, ripple,
stone, glittering arc of drops
from paddle blade
an invitation to calm
attention, reflection,
the spectators, as they gazed
at foot-float and elbow-glide,
leaf-flutter, feather-sheen,
spray and sparkle and swirl,
exclaiming to one another,
"This is everything!"

ANTHEM

In the dream
I was somehow able
through persistent focus and effort
to raise the level of something
to a threshold point
where it transcended
into something else —
such as ice to water,
stardust to life,
unrest to revolution.

As I woke, this dynamic
was attaching itself
to the noise machine
we use to blunt other sounds
from the street and upstairs apartment
and help us sleep.

Taking in the mechanical
hoarse, throaty drone,
as of sand or gravel
rasping over itself,
I began to hear faint
overtones, threads of high humming
that became more distinct
as I concentrated, and slowly
evolved into cosmic
harmonics, angelic choirings
tingling my head.

Several times recently
I've half-risen from dreams
in which I was working
on some concept or image

that seemed in some way related
to these Hemlock Gorge poems,
but, when I emerged far enough
to look at it closely
and try to approach it in words,
it seemed too abstract,
absurd, or irrelevant,
and melted away
as I drifted back into sleep.

But this has kept happening
as if some long-buried truth
from my paved-over unconscious,
of the species' collective one,
were trying to find expression,
and this morning I had the strong feeling
this one was for real,
so I got up at quarter-to-four
to write something down
before it slipped away,

and now, a few hours later, on Sitting Rock
I can see how it might relate
to this sequence of poems
in which I keep trying
to record and substantiate
some sense I have
of the sacredness and healing
depths of the gorge,
tucked away in the techno-buzz
of America,
so that others can hear,
above the relentless
grinding of our commercial
and military machines,
the delicate voices

of intersecting spheres:
an exquisite, polyphonic
terrestrial anthem.

FISH

At my first descent to the river
a fallen tree extends to the water's edge
where I've been perching in recent weeks
watching herons and cormorants
dragonflies and scooters
and the play of light, wind and water
at my feet,
full summer's cornucopia
brimming around me:
towering oak, pine and hemlock,
ripening berry and crabapple,
blooming yarrow, chicory
daisy, loosestrife and clover,
the air rich with creation's
swelling crescendo
of fragrance and flavor
color, caress and song.

Often in the sunlit shallows
a small brown fish
has come darting out of the depths
to cruise and hover
a few feet from my sneakers.
Slowly undulating
an elegant two-tiered tailfin
fringed with rippling silver,
she or he hangs just above
the pebbles and mossy sludge
that carpet the bottom,
facing me, then edging back and turning
to stare with a round black eye
rimmed with amber, a ruby dot toward the back,
her slim mud-brown torso
glowing with a faint crimson
translucence in the light,

now and then tilting sideways to reveal
a satiny rainbow sheen,
then shooting back into darkness
to reappear in a few seconds
a few feet to the left or right
and glide back to the spot right in front of me.

For weeks now I've been puzzling
over what she's doing there.
She doesn't appear to be feeding
marking or guarding some territory,
being courted or spawning —
perhaps, I've thought, she just comes
to bask in the sunlight
or take in the sky
or the curious ways of landfolk
or enjoy a few minutes
of fellow-creature companionship,
for she does seem as fascinated
by me as I am by her.

Then this morning, as I watched her
darting in, hovering, slipping back into darkness,
it occurred to me
that she was not simply observing me
or coming to cop a few rays,
but had been sent, an emissary
from all that is hidden, unknown,
to remind me how much there is
that I can't fathom,
so many elaborate works
of beauty and delicacy
billions of years in the crafting
that human hands have destroyed
in the last few hundred,
and countless more, still obscure,
that we are going to wipe out

if we're not much more careful…

and just as that thought swept through me,
a sharp slap and splashing
erupted downstream to my left,
and a voice yelled, "Hey Rich, I need help!"
I could see a large golden fish
flailing at each jerk, being slowly hauled in.
Then another shout from the unseen young man:
"Hey Rich, for real! I need help!
He's a big one! I donno what to do!"
Then a voice further downstream
across the little plank-bridge to Turtle Island
shot back, "I ain't comin' over there!"
A call and response evolved for several minutes:
urgent pleas and hurled scraps of advice
skimming across the water
to "wear 'im out!"
and "drag 'im up onto the bank!"

I didn't stay sitting long enough
to learn how it concluded,
recoiling from that frantic disconnect
of hooked man and fish.
The last I heard
as I made my way back up the gully
was, "Hey Rich, he's got a big mouth!
Should I hit 'im in the head with a stone?"

ONE

no thoughts this morning
just strolling, standing
sitting, breathing, being
with rock and river
bark, beam, chatter, flutter
open, absorbing, sensing
through shells the whole flowing
seamless, sacred
one

FISHER KING

Since April I've seen several candidates
for the wounded Fisher King,
but, aside from his ailing osprey
avian manifestation,
none has seemed archetypal, more
than some local dude out fishing
with no evident injury
spoiling his weekend fun

till this morning, in the midst
of a late July heatwave,
as I stood on the rock ledge
squinting into the sun,
the launched words of my mantra
wilting in air to drop
and slip like limp leaves
one by one over the falls,
then turned and beheld below me
not far from the roiling froth
a man in a gleaming boat
and knew it was him:

an old skinny black guy
with a gray pointed beard,
in jeans and, despite the day's mounting inferno,
a black wetsuit top,
perched on a crate
in a small aluminum outboard,
bent to the river, one hand propping his rod,
the other deftly winding or letting out line,
the boat adrift, turning slowly
in coils of yellow-brown foam.

I stood and watched him
reel in two empty hooks,

attach fresh bait, flick the line out again,
and resume his leaning posture
that exuded in the swelter
something of regal dignity and composure
through long adversity
and spoke to me of hope
and the wondrous resilience
of the human spirit.

Could his half-gallon plastic jug
be a present-day chalice?
or that battered pail contain
the mystic Grail?
Where is his wound? I looked closely,
then thought of the generations
of slavery, and the invisible
shackles and whips
of on-going prejudice
his people have suffered, endured.

What's he fishing for? I wondered,
this dispossessed, exiled monarch,
a crate for his throne —
and remembered reading at breakfast
about the prohibitive levels
of mercury now in all of Massachusetts'
fresh-water fish —
(Mercury, that old messenger,
come once again from the gods!) —
and the answer leapt up: reconnection
with the core and source: Mother Earth,
and, like all of us, survival
in waters poisoned by centuries
of myopic industrial fauxgress
and that potent blend of Yankee
ingenuity, gumption and greed.

VISION

This morning on Sitting Rock
when I opened my eyes
I saw between the leaves
somewhere off in the blue

poets stretch and shed
their brittle, nonreferential
postmodern skins
and evolve into visionary
dream-weavers of the future
global tribe…

I saw novelists break through
their ossified doomsday scowls
and absurdist smirks
and, smiling, conceive and create
a new kind of hero
who saves the day by losing
the big game, match, promotion
title bout, contract, or race,
perceiving, in an epiphanic moment,
the hostile opponent or rival
as a vulnerable fellow-
link in the cosmic chain…

I saw Hollywood turn
such tales into blockbusters
that had millions in tears
of empathic compassion
at the sweet jolt of each climax…

I saw TV reporters
pull back their probing
shock-proof lenses and mikes
from late-breaking open wounds,

buildings in flames, shattered
dreams and public careers,
and focus for half-an-hour
on a blade of grass thrusting
through concrete into the sun,
a seed in the wind,
a star pushing back darkness,
a wing and a petal
blending to one design,
to remind us that life,
for all its savagery, accidents, aberrations,
is a fabulous gift to dust
from some fathomless
originator's hand...

I saw couples and loving
self-pleasuring soloists
trade in the adrenaline rush
of the latest wasp-waisted siren
and tiger-tanked ram-tough models
for vintage tantric or Native
American vehicles
of ecstasy, riding for hours
in blissful surrender
the swell of orgasmic waves
sweeping higher and higher
until they bridged Earth and Heaven...

I saw spiritual anorexics,
suffering from the numb
empty restless boredom
of cosmic isolation and moral malaise,
rediscover in leaf and star
a sense of the sacred
and within themselves the boundless
interconnected universal flow
spiced with the charge

of consciousness and choice...

I saw nations vie with each other
to be the first
to eliminate the three Ps:
Poverty, Pollution, Prejudice,
directing the spirit and surge
of competition
toward a healing species-wide end...

I saw the sweet regreening
of a vast country,
blighted by hyper-consumption,
as more and more people
from all cultures and classes
slipped out of their 9-to-5
mass-produced, name-brand lives
and gathered in small-scale
co-op communities
whose M.O. was getting along
not getting ahead,
setting up websites and chatrooms
to brainstorm and swap techniques
such as boycotting fast-cash foodtroughs,
mummified supermarkets,
synthetic designer chains,
and prime time's ad-driven
stud-stomp-stud free-market ethos
of saving the world from itself
for democracy
or at least massive corporate profits;
planting trees, crops and gardens
in recycled parking lots
of abandoned malls;
creating need-based
neighborhood industries,
local stores, health clinics and schools

free of homogenizing
standardized tests;
finding plenty of time
to relax, read, talk, dream, walk,
watch the sun rise and set
in majestic mystery,
and play, dance and sing
in on-going festivals
celebrating the miracle
of being alive;
reflecting in disbelief
on how they could have worked
so long and so hard
for things they didn't need
or really want;
flying dove-spangled banners
of green, white and blue
from fossil-fuel-free
town halls, homes and cars
whose bumper stickers advised:
MAKE LOVE NOT MONEY
LIVE PEACE AND WAR WILL CEASE...

I saw the thing that doesn't love a wall
crumble international borders
all over the globe,
and a rising tide
of interracial and interreligious
friendships, couplings and offspring
till no one could tell or cared
who was what beyond human being.

Then a cloud crept over the blue,
and I saw more and more nations
flexing their nuclear biceps,
and multinational conglomerates,
backed by high-flying slogans and squadrons,

gutting and fouling the environment,
disrupting, exploiting, destroying
indigenous peoples and cultures;
and in revenge
a loose confederation
of tech-savvy third-world terrorists
toppling row after row of big business
skyscrapers like dominoes,
and felling millions of citizens
of the most powerful
vulnerable nation on Earth
with a few bombshells
stuffed with ancient plagues…

and a voice said, "There is still time
to turn back from the precipice
of self-extinction
and restore the modern wasteland.
Go now and tell your people
before it's too late!"

PICNIC

Here for an Indian Summer
Sunday picnic on Turtle Island
with Pat (former colleague and friend,
now wife and soulmate
of my silver years)
who introduced me to the gorge
a couple of summers ago
and has herself some threads
of Native blood
wound into her Irish/
Scotch/French Canadian skein

we loll in our beach chairs
lugged from the parking lot
by the lower falls
and munch and chat and reflect
about all that has gone on here
for millennia
and how, for the moment, time
seems to be on vacation
as we gaze up into the hemlocks'
evergreen
and check out a nuthatch
winding endlessly up and down
the trunk of returnity.

And after awhile
we haul our protesting
sixtyish bodies up
and go for a walk
down to the river, hoping to meet
the mallard pair we've encountered
on paddle-strolls of their own
or the integrated
native and lightfeather couple

I've told her about,
but all that greets us are shouts
from some kids under Echo Bridge
unaware of the ghostly
still-echoing bellows of thousands
from a century ago.

Then we hike up the bluff and along
the trail to Sitting Rock
where I brush off a few leaves
nutshells and crumbling turds
for my multinational Native
American sweetheart,
and we settle cozily in
on the ledge where Sits-on-a-Rock
and Praying Fox used to spoon
and she, more than once, on his lap
became Sits-on-a-Cock,
which we are not likely to mimic
here, in our sagging 60s,
well aware of the mores and laws
of our Puritan heritage
whose progeny still have a problem
dealing with that most natural
ecstatic act of creation
and if they discovered us at it
would haul us down to the station
for questioning, and slap us
with a stiff fine, or even
an unpleasant stint behind bars
to keep us from further damage
to a society
that savors a spoonful or two
of perversion with its coffee
each morning at breakfast.

So we just sit, holding hands,
and chat some more and gaze,
grateful there still exists
such a place to come to and be in
for an hour or two, softly floating
on the delicious sense
that nothing more needs to be done
than what we are doing,
as close to nirvana
Eden or Arcady
as we are likely to come.

Then we rouse ourselves
and make our way back to the lot
to drive back home to the list
of tasks that need tending to
before Monday morning hits
with its headlines of violence
and, back from my pre-dawn breakfast
and early ramble,
we plunge into the stream
of rushhour traffic to school
where I'll drop her off
and head for a coffee house
to work on the gleanings
from my walk in the gorge
often thinking I must be crazy
as well as wasting my time
to be trying to hold America's
past up to its present
in some healing way for its future.

What, after all, can I do
that might make any difference —
a poet working obscurely
to find words
to get at some elusive

inner itch
of experience, concept, vision
in a culture where such craft
gets lost in a glitzy sea
of hot-selling celebrity scandal
horror, soft-core romance
and dumbed-down, spandexed
platinum pop megastars —
still afloat and steering
by intuition's compass,
determined, attempting,
despite the odds, to reground
the consciousness of the tribe
in the miraculousness
and cosmic interconnectedness
of existence?

What can I do, at this point
but keep muddling and marveling
my way along 61
with Pat at my side,
and my two grown sons
who come over most weeks
for pizza and beer and an evening's
exchange of intimacies
about our evolving
cosmologies, traumas and hopes,
and my weekly café musings
and jazz-duo sessions
with a precious handful of soulfriends
who honor my dreams and dilemmas?

What can I do
but keep hoping, urging
the serpentine river
of humanity
not to turn on itself in a blind

self-devouring frenzy,
but to turn and turn on itself
in Ourobourian rounds of contemplation
of where we've all come from,
where we are at the moment,
and where we might go from here?

What can I do
but keep moving, musing and writing
whatever I can't not write
as best I can, sending out
my plain-speaking, sensuous
sometimes wonderwhelmed voice,
and think of it as a drop
that, mingling with others,
makes up the cosmic ocean,
a vibration pulsing
extending, endlessly
to be picked up someday,
considered, absorbed, recast
in some cutting-edge cyberpoetic,
and issued worldwebwide
to inspire the times
by some fresh new-millennial quester
who, venturing boldly
around the entire planet,
has come upon the holy
healing Grail,
not in the depths
of some raging modern inferno,
or up on some spell-shrouded peak,
but sitting, refulgent
with dew-jeweled light
for anyone to claim
a few steps
from countless woodland paths
on a rock?

DREAM

I dreamed I was hiding
behind a rock,
peeking over the top
at a bomb buried nearby
that was set to go off.
A red light flashed on
and I ducked down and braced myself.
I didn't hear anything,
but the stone began to warm
and press against me —
I could feel its rough skin
and muscles rippling beneath.
The heat kept building and building
until my whole body seemed molten,
seething with fear
and unexpected pleasure,
and I couldn't tell
if the bomb, the rock, or myself
was going to explode.

I woke to find myself soaked
and tingling from toes to scalp,
my penis spasming
on the verge of release,
at home in bed
with Pat sleeping beside me,
thinking thank God
I'm not about to die!
But instead of easing
back from the dream
I opened into it
to see where it would take me,
and lay there curled
feeling well and surge through me
again and again,

as stone turned to flesh
and flesh to ecstasy,
the sweet, terrifying lava
of transformation.

AUTHOR

Douglas Worth was born in 1940 and grew up in Pennsylvania, Florida, and India. He has been writing poetry since the seventh grade, attempting for half a century to express his sense of the miraculousness of existence and the rich weave of human joy and suffering, his growing concern with modern humanity's disrespect for Nature, and his deepening conviction of universal interconnectedness. He taught English at public and private schools in Manhattan and Newton, Massachusetts, from 1965 to1990, after which he retired to devote himself to writing and playing jazz alto sax. Worth lives with his artist wife Patricia and their half-wild cat in Cambridge, Mass. Ranging in scope from the intimate personal, through the geo-political, to the cosmic, Douglas Worth's poetry has been published widely in periodicals and anthologies, and he has received a number of fellowships, grants, and prizes, and been profiled in *Who's Who in America, Contemporary Authors, and The International Who's Who in Poetry*. Hailed by historian Howard Zinn as "a visionary dream-weaver of the future global tribe," Worth has been termed "an American poet who counts" by novelist Hugh Nissenson, who concludes that his "unique lyric vernacular voice marks him simultaneously as a confessional — and yes, transcendental — poet, whose work I believe is destined to endure."

In addition to his volumes of poetry, Worth is the author of a young-adult novella and an illustrated children's book. His published works are:

Of Earth, William L. Bauhan, 1974
Invisibilities, Apple-wood Press, 1977
Triptych, Apple-wood Press, 1979
From Dream, From Circumstance, Apple-wood Books, 1984
Once Around Bullough's Pond, William L. Bauhan, 1987
Some Sense of Transcendence, William L. Bauhan, 1999
Echoes in Hemlock Gorge, Higganum Hill Books, 2003
Deerfoot's Mile, Creative Arts Book Company, 2003
Grumpy the Christmas Cat, MightyBook, 2003
Catch the Light, Higganum Hill Books, 2004